We Built A Family Together

The History of the Parish of the Assumption of the Blessed Virgin Mary

Morristown, New Jersey

by Jeanette C. and Robert J. Fredericks

Layout and Design by Tivoli Creative Design Studio, Madison, NJ
Printed by Signature Book Printing www.sbpbooks.com

Contents

DIOCESE OF PATERSON

Diocesan Center
777 Valley Road
Clifton, New Jersey 07013

Office of
THE BISHOP

(973) 777-8818   Fax (973) 777-8976

June 2011

My Dear Friends in Christ,

What a great honor it is to be asked to include a letter for "The History of the Parish of the Church of the Assumption". Assumption Parish is such a wonderful Catholic community filled with people who practice their faith in both word and deed.

The Catechism of the Catholic Church describes the parish as a place that "initiates the Christian people into the ordinary expression of the liturgical life: it gathers them together in this celebration; it teaches Christ's saving doctrine; it practices the charity of the Lord in good works and brotherly love."

Over these past decades, Assumption Parish has been a place where the people have come to know Jesus more personally in the breaking of the bread. Our Diocese is blessed to have such a vibrant and Eucharistic people in our midst!

A special word of thanks goes to Robert and Jeanette Fredericks for undertaking the task of updating Father Flynn's "The Story of a Parish." I have no doubt that Assumption Parish's best days lie ahead with additional chapters of faith in action waiting to be written.

Faithfully yours in Christ,

+ Arthur J. Serratelli

Most Reverend Arthur J. Serratelli, S.T.D., S.S.L., D.D.
Bishop of Paterson

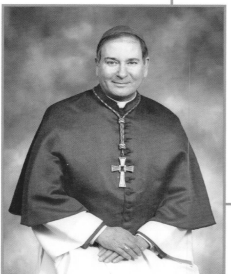

ASSUMPTION PARISH

Community · History · Spirituality

Dear Parishioners,

With great joy I present *We Built A Family Together*, written by our parishioners, Robert and Jeanette Fredericks. This book is the culmination of their labor of love over the past two years.

French writer Alexis de Tocqueville, after visiting America in 1831, said, "I sought for the greatness of the United States in her commodious harbors, her ample rivers, her fertile fields, and boundless forests–and it was not there. I sought for it in her rich mines, her vast world commerce, her public school system, and in her institutions of higher learning–and it was not there. I looked for it in her democratic Congress and her matchless Constitution–and it was not there. Not until I went into the churches of America and heard her pulpits flame with righteousness did I understand the secret of her genius and power. America is great because America is good, and if America ever ceases to be good, America will cease to be great!"

The Church of the Assumption of the Blessed Virgin Mary, founded in 1848, typifies the kind of church of which the famous historian wrote. Our history is replete with sterling examples of parishioners, priests, and religious who have labored together to spread the Gospel and live their Catholic faith with great fervor and devotion in this portion of the Lord's vineyard, Morristown, New Jersey.

It is an honor to serve here with you and witness first-hand your enthusiastic love of Jesus Christ manifested in the many facets of this splendid parish. I am certain that you will enjoy reading about our predecessors whose adventures in evangelization provided the foundations of our parish life and inspire us as we serve the Lord in the twenty-first century and into the future.

With prayers and congratulations, I remain

Sincerely yours in Christ,

Fr. John

Rev. Msgr. John E. Hart
Pastor

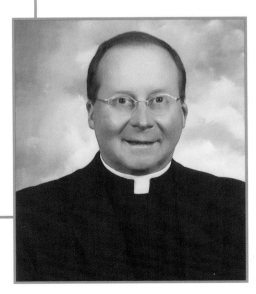

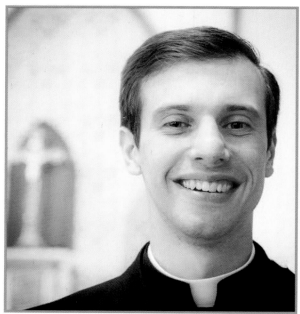

© Sergio Burani—Photos by Sergio

Rev. Philip-Michael Tangorra
Associate Pastor at Assumption
July 1, 2011, to Present

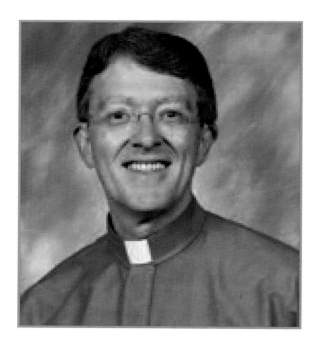

Rev. Dennis J. Crowley
Associate Pastor at Assumption
June 1, 1999, through June 30, 2011

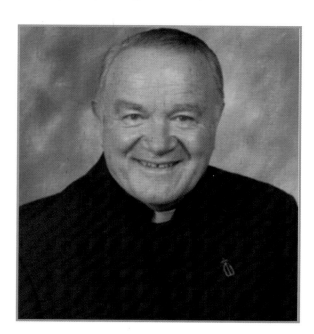

Rev. Msgr. Martin F. Rauscher
Pastor Emeritus

Acknowledgments

We owe heartfelt gratitude to the following for their cooperation and services in helping us to gather countless facts, dates, and vignettes and to transform them into an engaging narrative of a remarkable Catholic parish:

To those parishioners who so willingly shared their personal stories and memorabilia of life in a younger, ever-evolving Assumption parish;

To Liz Wilkey and the members of her administrative staff who made accessible to us parish files, archives, and several dusty boxes in the rectory basement that held a treasure trove of information;

To Cheryl Turkington, Assistant Archivist at the North Jersey History Center of the Morristown & Morris Township Library, for the photograph of "The Beehive" and her insight and knowledge of "Little Dublin";

To Sergio Burani, for his artistry and skill at capturing the quintessence of light and angle in order to maximize the beauty and drama of his photographs;

To Monsignor Martin F. Rauscher for his patient answers to our endless questions about the Assumption of his youth, the Assumption of his pastorate, and almost everything in between;

To Monsignor Raymond J. Kupke, PhD, who reviewed this work for liturgical and historical accuracy; and to Karen Ann Kurlander, who served as proofreader and copy editor for literary precision;

And to Monsignor John E. Hart, Pastor of the Church of the Assumption, for his foresight and vision in allowing this parish history to be written. We hope this narrative will serve both as a reminder of the significant role Assumption has played in the evolution of this community, and as an important resource for the 200th anniversary of this splendid parish in the year 2048, thirty-seven years from this day.

Jeanette and Robert Fredericks
August 15, 2011

the CHURCH

Dedicated to

- *the early Catholics of the Morristown area who fought and worked for the practice of the Catholic religion despite flagrant prejudice, abject poverty, and other hardships;*

- *those who established and maintained Assumption Church, which later became the mother of neighboring Catholic parishes and institutions;*

- *and those who today continue to enjoy, maintain, and enlarge this great inheritance called the Church of the Assumption of the Blessed Virgin Mary in Morristown, New Jersey.*

lthough Assumption officially dates from 1848, it can be argued that its establishment as a parish was built upon the early history and tradition of the Catholics in New Jersey going back to the early days of New Jersey—indeed before there was a State of New Jersey.

In colonial New Jersey, Catholics were few in number. In the late 1600s, Catholics were known to have settled in Woodbridge during the administration of Governor Thomas Dongan, himself a Catholic. At this time, the few Catholics living in the Jerseys (East and West Jersey) were permitted to practice their faith. Indeed, a Jesuit, Father Thomas Harvey, was known to have visited Woodbridge and Elizabethtown, the capital of East Jersey, and, no doubt, celebrated Mass there. However, Governor Dongan was removed from office in 1691. This led to the passage of anti-Catholic legislation. In 1698, the East Jersey Assembly enacted a law providing that no professed Christians would be molested, punished, or disturbed, "…providing this shall not extend to any of the Romish religion the right to exercise their manner of worship contrary to the laws and statutes of England," (Flynn, *The Catholic Church in New Jersey*, p.12). On September 16, 1701, a law was passed by the Assembly of New York by which "papists and popish recusants are prohibited from voting for members of the Assembly or for any office whatsoever, from thenceforth and forever" (Flynn, *The Catholic Church in New Jersey*, p.8). When New Jersey became a royal colony in 1702, Queen Anne in her instructions to the new Royal Govennor, Lord Cornbury, permitted liberty of conscience to everyone except papists (Kupke, p.4). We shall see that this anti-Catholic sentiment was to persist in New Jersey and indeed in Morristown for years to come.

(opposite page)
Interior of the Church of the Assumption, March, 2011.
© *Sergio Burani—Photos by Sergio*

The first Church of the Assumption, constructed in 1848.

100th Anniversary, Church of the BVM, p.13

Nevertheless, Catholics continued to arrive in New Jersey. It is estimated that by the time of the American Revolution and indeed during Washington's second encampment in Morristown (1779-1780), there were several hundreds of Irish Catholics among Washington's troops. This resulted in Washington recognizing the contributions of his Irish troops to the cause of the Revolution. On March 16, 1780, "General Orders issued to the Troops encamped at Morristown" stated that in recognition of the "…brave and generous people" of Ireland and "…their operation to promote the cause of America…the General directs that all Fatigue and working parties cease tomorrow [March] the seventeenth, a day held in Particular regard by the people of that Nation." It was further stated that the "Commanding Officer desires that the celebration of this day not pass by without having a little Rum issued to the troops…"(Flynn, *Story of a Parish*, pp.22-23).

It was also during the Revolution that the first Catholic Mass may have been celebrated in Morristown in the Ford Mansion, Washington's Headquarters. On April 19, 1779, Don Juan de Miralles, a Spanish agent, was stricken with pulmonary trouble; he died on April 28. The chaplain of the French Ambassador, the Rev. Seraphin Bandol, hurried on from Philadelphia and administered the last rites to the dying Spaniard in the Ford Mansion and may have celebrated Mass there.

Following the Revolution and the creation of our country, the Irish who remained in Morris County only occasionally saw a Catholic priest. They were married by a squire or a magistrate and drifted away from the church. Many of the Celtic names in Morristown in the first quarter of the 19th Century had lost their distinctive character. Thus, McGee became Magee; McCarthy became Mccarty; Callahan, Callinan, and so forth.

Nevertheless, Catholic influence did grow in New Jersey. As a result of the French Revolution and the rise of Napoleon, a number of French aristocrats had settled in the Caribbean and subsequently by 1805 emigrated to Madison, then known as Bottle Hill. This led to the creation of the Church of Saint Vincent in Madison, perhaps as early as 1834.

Other than the above-mentioned Mass that may have been celebrated in the Ford Mansion, the first Mass celebrated in Morristown was perhaps in 1845. Unfortunately, the location of that Mass is in dispute. The pastor of Saint Vincent's in 1847, Father Louis Dominic Senez, purchased land for $400 to build the first Catholic church in Morristown. The lot was at the location where our rectory now stands. Father Bernard McQuaid, the pastor of Saint Vincent's in Madison from 1848 to 1853 and of the Morristown mission, built the first Catholic church in Morristown. It was dedicated on August 15, 1848, the feast of the Assumption of the Blessed Virgin Mary and named in her honor. On Christmas Day, 1848, Mass was celebrated for the first time in the new church. According to Father Flynn in his book *The Story of a Parish*, the altar was merely wooden planks on barrels. There were no pews or kneeling benches. The congregation consisted of some forty to seventy people, including a fair number of Protestants, for that first Mass.

It is interesting to note that Father Senez had purchased a crucifix and candleholders for the main altar. When Father Senez was reassigned to Saint Patrick's Cathedral in Newark, Mrs. William Collins and Mrs. John Rogers went door to door to raise $60 to purchase the items from Father Senez. In his book, *The Story of a Parish*, Father Flynn reports that the same crucifix surmounted the tabernacle on the high altar as late as 1892 and the candleholders were used for Requiem Masses. We believe that this same crucifix and candleholders currently grace our sanctuary.

On March 5, 1849, Bishop John Hughes, the Bishop of New York whose jurisdiction then included New Jersey, dedicated the church. The building was a plain, frame structure with a basement. It measured 58 by 38 feet and could

This is the crucifix believed to have been purchased by Father Senez. It currently rests atop the tabernacle in the sanctuary.

© *Sergio Burani—Photos by Sergio*

accommodate 300. The parishioners by this time numbered 120. The first sexton was Mr. William O'Toole who was paid fifty cents per week.

Realizing the importance of education in the Catholic faith, Father McQuaid soon established a school in the basement of the church. In 1850 Saint Mary's School opened with twenty five children in attendance. Today, our historic school, now known as Assumption School, is the second oldest continuously functioning Catholic school in New Jersey.

The first teacher at Saint Mary's school was a Mr. Tracey of New York. Apparently, he was a stern taskmaster who believed in the concept "spare the rod and spoil the child" *(Flynn, Story of a Parish, p.47)*.

Father McQuaid must have been an extraordinary man. He traveled throughout his extensive parish on horseback, the reins in one hand and his breviary in the other. His parish stretched from Millburn and Springfield through Morristown, Dover, Stanhope, Waterloo, Newton, Boonton, Hanover, and Whippany, totaling about 120 Catholics, as noted above. Covering so large an area proved such a physical challenge that he was occasionally observed asleep in the saddle with his horse safely retracing their way home *(Flynn, Story of a Parish, p. 40)*.

In 1853, New Jersey was separated from the New York Diocese and elevated to the dignity of a diocese of its own. Appointed the first bishop was James Roosevelt Bailey, a convert to the Catholic Church and the nephew of Elizabeth Bayley Seton, better known as Mother Seton. Bishop Bayley then purchased the Chegarray School, a boarding school for girls and a property of one of the original emigres from the French West Indies. It was here that he opened Seton Hall College and appointed Father McQuaid as its first president, thus ending Father McQuaid's association with Assumption. Father McQuaid was subsequently to become the first bishop of Rochester, New York, and Seton Hall would be moved to its present location in South Orange, New Jersey.

Father McQuaid was succeeded by the Rev. Michael Madden who continued to be in charge of both Assumption and Saint Vincent's in Madison. Father Madden was to remain as pastor* at Assumption for four years, from 1853 to 1857.

---

* *Author's Note: Technically, Fathers Senez, McQuaid, and Madden were not "pastors" at Assumption, which was still a mission church and did not have a "pastor." However, we have followed the convention employed at Assumption; namely, that the first pastor was Father Senez.*

Father Madden was succeeded by Father Lawrence Hoey, the first priest to reside permanently in Morristown. In 1860, the Morristown Mission was separated from Madison. Since there was not as yet a residence for priests in Morristown, Father Hoey stayed at the residence of Mrs. Julia Rogers, located on James Street (then named New Vernon Road) for eleven months while trying to build a rectory. His efforts were rewarded when in 1861 a lot was purchased for $150, and construction began. Father Hoey also purchased from William Collins for $500 what was to become the original graveyard. Father Hoey continued the support of Saint Mary's School. A number of lay teachers were hired over the years, succeeding Mr. Tracey. During times of a vacancy, Father Hoey, himself an educator, pitched in and taught at the school. In 1865, the school could no longer accommodate the number of students desiring admittance and was consequently enlarged at a cost of $800.

Other Catholic enclaves began to emerge in the area. On September 29, 1859, the Order of the Sisters of Charity of Saint Elizabeth was established in Newark, relocating on July 2, 1860, to what was then known as the Village of Madison in Chatham Township and occupying the former Chegarray School for girls. In 1866 an Assumption Mission, Saint James, was founded in Basking Ridge.

Unfortunately, anti-Catholic bigotry was never far beneath the surface. It was not unusual in Morristown, around the time of the celebration of Saint Patrick's Day, to see a stuffed figure representing Saint Patrick suspended from a flagpole or a tree with a string of potatoes around the neck, a whiskey bottle in one pocket and a codfish in the other.

In July of 1867, the Rev. James D'Arcy was appointed pastor. Father D'Arcy was to serve for only one year. However, during that time he did establish temperance societies, religious sodalities and the cadet society for boys 10 to 18.

Father D'Arcy was succeeded by Father Patrick McGovern in 1868, who served as pastor until 1871. He took a conservative approach to parish finances, paying off the parish debt.

The parish had been growing to the point that the church building could no longer accommodate the parishioners. The crowds attending Mass filled the entire church and overflowed onto the steps leading into the church and onto the street. Father McGovern's parishioners talked to him about constructing a new church, but to no avail. He was adamantly opposed to incurring any kind of debt. He

A lithograph of the exterior of the newly constructed Church of the Assumption. It is the earliest known representation of the newly constructed church. The building behind the church is the first rectory which was subsequently used as a convent for the Sisters of Charity.

G.H.Walker and Company, Boston

resigned the pastorate in the autumn of 1871 and was succeeded by Father James Sheeran in October of the same year.

Father Sheeran was another remarkable man. Born in Ireland in 1819, he emigrated to Canada at the age of twelve and two years later to New York City. He married and had two children, a boy and a girl. After his wife died in 1849, he joined the Redemptorist Congregation and was ordained to the priesthood in 1858. He was assigned to New Orleans in 1861 and became an ardent believer in the Confederate cause. During the Civil War, he served as a Confederate chaplain. The story is told that, during the battle of the Shenandoah Valley, he attempted to advise General "Stonewall" Jackson as to how to proceed with the battle with the Union forces. General Jackson replied, "Father Sheeran, who will be responsible for this battle, Father Sheeran or General Jackson?" (Flynn, *Story of a Parish*, p. 71).

Following the war, as a result of a disagreement with his Redemptorist superior, Father Sheeran was permitted to withdraw from that Order. He was adopted by Bishop Bayley for the Diocese of Newark, and in 1871 he became pastor at Assumption. The question of a new church for the Assumption community was raised immediately. Fortunately, because of the foresight of Father McQuaid, a lot was available next to the existing church on the corner of Maple Avenue and Madison Street. It was being used as the church burial ground. The dead buried at this site were reverently disinterred and buried elsewhere (presumably adjacent to the then-existing cemetery on the church grounds). The plans for the construction of a new church were developed and bids were put out. The winning bid called for a cost of $37,000, exclusive of the sanctuary windows and altars. On June 30, 1872, the cornerstone was laid and blessed by Bishop Bayley. *The Morrisown Republican* reported that the Delaware, Lackawanna and Western Railroad sent a special train from New York that arrived about noon carrying some one hundred persons including priests from the monastery of the Passionist Fathers at Hoboken, the clergy of Seton Hall College and the Saint Elizabeth Convent. It was reported that a total of 3,000 people were present for the ceremony. Thus was born the present church building.

To allow Father Sheeran to devote his full energies to the construction of the new church, the missions of Basking Ridge and Mendham, which had been conducted out of Assumption, were assigned their own pastors at this time.

On Ascension Thursday, May 22, 1873, our new church was solemnly blessed by Bishop Michael Corrigan. A Solemn Pontifical Mass followed the blessing. During the Mass, music was rendered by a choir made up of members selected from the different churches in Newark.

The church is built of brick trimmed with sandstone. It is 120 feet in length and 52 feet in breadth. Its style borders on the Gothic.

The interior of the church, pre-1892. This is the earliest known representation of the Church's interior.

The Story of a Parish, p.74

The former church building was then altered for the accommodation of school children. The teaching staff at this time included Miss Maggie O'Brien, Miss Susan Coxe for the girls, and Mr. Coyle for the boys.

In September of 1875, as a result of the growth of vocations to the Sisters of Charity of Saint Elizabeth, Father Sheeran asked for two sisters to be sent from the motherhouse in Convent Station to serve at Assumption School. A little room was added to the school with a stove and cupboard. Thus was established the close association of the Sisters of Charity with Assumption School, which continues to this day.

The burial ground adjacent to the church was now at full capacity, and it became necessary to look for a new cemetery. In the spring of 1875, some sixteen acres of pastoral grounds, located about a mile from the church, were purchased. This was to become Holy Rood Cemetery.

Father Sheeran was a man with strong views. His ten years as pastor at Assumption were "stormy." His stern demeanor and determined ways often irritated his assistants and parishioners. On at least two occasions, Bishop Corrigan met with the parishioners to calm troubled waters.

Father Sheeran's health had been deteriorating for some time. He died on April 3, 1881, at the age of sixty-eight and was buried at Holy Rood Cemetery in a plot he had selected. During his pastorate, the present church building was constructed, Holy Rood Cemetery was established, and the first rectory was enlarged.

Father Sheeran was succeeded by Father Joseph Michael Flynn in June of 1881. During Father Flynn's long pastorate, which lasted into the 20th Century, many improvements in the church building and in the parish were made, some of which continue to have a positive impact on the quality of life in the greater Morristown community today.

Joseph Flynn was born in Springfield, Massachusetts, on January 7, 1848. At the age of sixteen, he enlisted in the New Jersey Volunteers and saw military service in the Civil War. It is interesting that he and his predecessor, Father Sheeran, were on opposite sides during this conflict. He was ordained to the priesthood at the seminary at Seton Hall College on May 30, 1874. On June 15, 1881, he became the pastor at Assumption.

One of Father Flynn's first activities at Assumption was to obtain a bell for the church tower.

The monument in Holy Rood Cemetery marking the burial place of Father Sheeran.

© Sergio Burani—Photos by Sergio

Father Flynn felt that having a bell would ensure that his congregation would arrive for Mass on time! He traveled to Baltimore to consult with McShane and Company which had just cast a bell for the Atlanta Exposition. However, the managers of the Atlanta Exposition had changed their minds and no longer wanted the bell. It was offered to Father Flynn for the price of the metal—$654.48. The bell, which weighed 2,477 pounds, was installed at Assumption and blessed by Bishop Winand Wigger, then the Bishop of Newark, on October 19, 1881. Very appropriately for the many parishioners of Irish descent at Assumption, the bell was named Saint Patrick. Saint Patrick continues to toll for various church functions at Assumption to this day.

The number of Catholics in Morris Plains and the surrounding area was increasing. Also, there was a need to minister to Catholics at Greystone, the state hospital for the mentally impaired. To satisfy these needs, Father Flynn purchased property in Morris Plains. On October 15, 1882, he laid the cornerstone for a new

Saint Mary's Young Men's Catholic Association building on South Street, Morristown. Since 1919 this structure has been the home of the George Washington Council of the Knights of Columbus.

Story of a Parish, p.190

church in Morris Plains, and on Christmas Day Mass was celebrated in the new church dedicated to Saint Virgil, a medieval bishop of Salzburg. It was the first church in the United States dedicated to this saint. Saint Virgil, or more formally, Saint Virgilius, was a son of Ireland who emigrated to France about the year 743 and eventually to Salzburg where he was named archbishop. He was noted for his great learning and was canonized in 1233.

On December 13, 1886, a larger site was purchased at the junction of Mountain Way and Hanover and Speedwell Avenues—Saint Virgil's present location. This site would allow for a future church, school, and rectory to be in proximity. In August of 1888, the church was moved to the new location, which comprises more than two acres. A belfry and gallery were added.

On September 6, 1881, Thomas Burns, an Assumption parishioner, donated his home directly in front of the church on the northwest corner of Madison Street and Maple Avenue to Father Flynn for the fee of one dollar. Father Flynn in turn deeded this property to the Church for one dollar on August 26, 1882. This became a residence for the Sisters of Charity who taught at Saint Mary's School. The sisters occupied that convent in January of 1882.

One of Father Flynn's striking innovations was the creation of the Young Men's Catholic Association. Composed of young men who were described as "mechanics," the Association was born in the autumn of 1881 with twenty-six members. No doubt, this initiative was of great value to these young men in the not-always-friendly environment shown to young Catholics in Morristown. It provided an opportunity for them to get together, enjoy each other's company and, on occasion, invite the young ladies of the parish to join them for a social evening. Many of these young men were later to relate that these were the brightest and happiest days that they had ever known.

However, the Young Men's Catholic Association lacked one important component to make the organization complete—its own home. This was remedied when Father Flynn obtained a lot on South Street. For $25,000, which included the cost of the lot, a handsome building was constructed and dedicated on May 1, 1888. The building still stands today and is the proud headquarters of the George Washington Council of the Knights of Columbus.

To commemorate the life and accomplishments of the late pastor, Father Sheeran, the Rosary Society placed a memorial window in the church. Patrick

The Monstrance.

Farrelly and his wife, benefactors of the parish, placed windows in the Lady Chapel (formerly located on the right side of the church, as one faces the altar) in memory of their deceased children. These windows were produced by Mayer and Company of Munich, Germany, and, according to Father Flynn, were the first such products shipped across the Atlantic from this renowned firm.

Mrs. Farrelly generously donated the sanctuary lamp and Miss Ann Hogan the ostensorium (a monstrance), both of which were purchased in Lyons, France.

It is interesting to note that music was always part of Assumption's liturgy. Father Flynn, in his book *The Story of a Parish*, mentioned that a "little organ" was placed in the choir loft at the dedication of the Church. This was replaced in 1884 by a much larger organ costing $1,500 and built by E. and G.G. Hook of Boston for a Protestant church. This was but one of several organs to grace our church during its long history.

Congregational singing had not been part of Assumption's tradition. However, following the Third Plenary Council of Bishops in 1884, the congregation was encouraged to take a more active part in church ritual. Father Flynn encouraged his parishioners to sing hymns at Benediction and during the Stations of the Cross during Lent, with great success.

Morristown and the number of Catholics in the town continued to grow in numbers. Assumption's parishioners were spread out throughout the town. Because of this, when the weather was inclement, many could not attend Mass. For some time, the Condit property, consisting of almost ten acres and located at the junction of Sussex and Speedwell Avenues, was up for sale. After considerable thought, the property was purchased by Father Flynn for $25,000.

The property was divided into building lots, and the lots auctioned. Streets were laid out and named: Columba, in honor of the great saint of Iona; Grant, in honor of the general of the Union forces during the Civil War who was then dying; and Bellevue Terrace, named for the view accorded from this street. These streets continue to be in use to this day.

A lot was set aside for a new church, and on May 31, 1885, the cornerstone was laid for the first church building on this site. The church was named in honor of Saint Margaret of Scotland, who was held in high devotion by those of Celtic extraction. As with Saint Virgil, Saint Margaret of Scotland was recognized for the first time on a church building in the United States. The church of Saint Margaret of Scotland, a simple building, was constructed for $1,000.

As noted previously, the first Saint Mary's school was established in the basement of the first Assumption Church building. With the construction of the new Assumption Church, the old church building was modified and used as the school. As the parish continued to grow, it was apparent that a new and larger school would have to be constructed. On March 29, 1886, Father Flynn announced that a new school building was to be constructed on the site of the old cemetery. The remains buried there were carefully disinterred and moved to the new cemetery, Holy Rood.

Construction of the new school commenced. Bishop McQuaid of Rochester, who had been the second pastor at Assumption, was invited back to speak at the laying of the cornerstone of the school, which he did on Thanksgiving Day, November 25, 1886. Bishop Winand Wigger of the Diocese of New Jersey, and himself a former pastor at the Church of Saint Vincent, Madison, blessed the cornerstone. On September 19, 1887, the children took possession of their new school, which was joyfully blessed by Bishop Wigger on October 2, 1887*. The new school was built of brick with granite trim. The first floor contained six classrooms, and the basement held a recreation room. The school also had a hall with a stage. The school at that time was still referred to as the "Saint Mary's Parish School." It was subsequently to be renamed "The Bayley School" after Bishop Bayley of Newark.

In 1890, Father Flynn announced that he had sold the sisters' residence for $4,000 and that he intended to build a new rectory on the site of the first church. When the construction of the new rectory was complete, the sisters would occupy the old rectory located on Madison Street. The construction of the rectory was begun on March 22, 1890, and on November 25 the priests took possession.

The growth of Morristown led Father Flynn to the realization that a hospital was needed to care for the sick, injured, and infirm. In November of 1881, within the octave of the feast day of All Souls, the concept of a hospital was again raised.

There was the thought that possibly the Grey Nuns of Montréal, who specialized in hospital work, could be induced to come to Morristown. After some negotiation, the Grey Nuns agreed to take on the challenge. The Arnold Tavern, Washington's Headquarters during his first encampment in Morristown in 1777, had been purchased by Julia Keese Colles in 1886 and moved from the Green to her estate on Mt. Kemble Avenue. In 1892, the Arnold Tavern was purchased by the All Souls Hospital Association, and All Souls Hospital commenced operations later that year. All Souls Hospital would remain an active Catholic hospital until February 1970. The building would eventually be purchased by Morristown Memorial Hospital. **

* Authors' Note: Records agree that September 19, 1887, was the first day of classes at the new St. Mary's School. However, a discrepancy occurs regarding the date of its blessing. The official program lists October 2, 1887; Father Flynn records a date of October 9, 1887, in his history The Story of a Parish.

**Authors' Note: Morristown Memorial Hospital is now known as The Morristown Medical Center.

The Bayley School (Saint Mary's Parish School), pre-1892.

1972 Assumption Custom Book, p.19

The present rectory, circa 1891. Note that Maple Avenue is still a dirt road.

Story of a Parish, p.229

During Father Flynn's long pastorate, improvements continued to be made on the newly constructed church. In 1875, the statue of the Sacred Heart was placed on the Gospel side (that is, the left side as one faces the altar) of the High Altar (the High Altar was subsequently removed during the pastorate of Monsignor Dericks), and on June 18, 1882, the statue of Saint Anthony of Padua, given by Mrs. Patrick Welsh in memory of her son John Vincent, was installed on the Epistle side. Also in the 1880s additional stained glass windows were donated and installed in the church. In 1907, Mr. and Mrs. Louis A. Thebaud donated a marble statue of Our Lady of the Assumption which was imported from Italy. Mrs. Patrick Welsh in 1887

donated the statue of the Pieta, which had been fabricated by Mayer and Company of Munich. Photographs of many of these artifacts are displayed in The Art section of this publication.

In the 1880s, the first of many redecorations of the church occurred. The walls and panels were painted in light colors of salmon and blue with the reeds painted brown and olive green. Wilton carpeting was laid on the wooden floor of the sanctuary and in the side chapels.

In March 17, 1886, the accomplishments of Father Flynn were recognized when he was made the Dean (a priest appointed to oversee a group of parishes within a diocese) of Morris and Sussex Counties.

In 1887, the Ambassador of the Austro-Hungarian Empire, representing Salzburg, sent a relic of Saint Virgil, which was placed on the High Altar. Other gifts included a sanctuary lamp, adoring angels placed on the High Altar, and a silver ciborium. In 1887, the Stations of the Cross, given by the Farrelly family, were placed on the walls where they remain to this day. The stations are painted on copper and were obtained from Carbane of Paris, France.

The Rosary Society, the oldest organization in the parish, was established in 1875. The Holy Name Society was formally established at Assumption in 1886 and remained active until the 1960s. Also in the 1880s, the Children of Mary, the League of the Sacred Heart, and the Apostolate of Prayer were important organizations in the spiritual life of the parish. Because of changing lifestyles, these organizations have ceased to exist. On July 8, 1898, Father Flynn organized the George Washington Council of the Knights of Columbus. The Knights would take possession of the Young Men's Catholic Association building on South Street in 1919 where they remain active to this day.

In 1889, electricity arrived at the Church of the Assumption. For $750, an electrical system provided by D. Lim was installed in the church, providing lighting year-round and replacing the previously used gas jets.

In 1907, toward the end of the long and productive pastorate of Father Flynn, *The Parish Review*, "the official organ of the Church of the Assumption, Morristown" was established. *The Parish Review* would continue to be published monthly until at least 1948.

Father Flynn's health had been deteriorating for some time. On January 5, 1910, this dynamic pastor went home to the Lord. During his twenty-nine years as pastor of the Church of the Assumption, Father Flynn improved the adornment of the newly constructed church, constructed the new Bayley School and established the Bayley High School, constructed the present rectory on Maple Avenue, established Saint Margaret's Church and School and Saint Virgil's Church, established the Young Men's Catholic Association, built that organization's building on South Street, and founded All Souls Hospital. In addition, the history that he wrote, *The Story of a Parish, 1847-1892*, is the oldest history of a Catholic parish in the State of New Jersey. He later wrote *The Catholic Church in New Jersey*. What a remarkable legacy of accomplishment!

Father Flynn was succeeded by Father George Brown, who was installed as pastor on January 31, 1910. Father Brown held the dual appointment of rector of Saint Margaret's Church as well as the Assumption pastorate and on June 22, 1911, was appointed Dean of Morris and Sussex Counties. In 1912, Father Brown purchased property on the southeast corner of Maple Avenue and Madison Street from Miss T. F. Clifford for $6,000. The objective of the purchase was to prevent the erection of anything unsightly which would detract from the Church of the Assumption.

Father Brown had been in ill health for some time. His tenure at Assumption was cut short by his sudden death in 1914. He was succeeded by Father Edward J. Ellard who was appointed pastor at Assumption on August 9, 1914. Father Ellard was to serve at Assumption as its pastor for twenty-three years.

Edward J. Ellard was born in New York City. While he was young, his family moved to Paterson, New Jersey, where he attended school. He was an outstanding athlete in football and baseball at Seton Hall and was especially skilled as a boxer. He frequently gave boxing exhibitions at Bayley Hall in the Bayley School in Morristown. He was ordained in the Diocese of Newark by Bishop Wigger on June 12, 1897, and served in various parishes, including as pastor at Saint Virgil's in Morris Plains for two years. A splendid horseman, he rode daily around town on his horse, often with the Reverend John C. Lord of Saint Peter's Episcopal Church, with his dog trailing behind.

Parishioners who lived along James Street, Macculloch Avenue, and Madison Street looked forward to talking to Father Ellard as he strolled by in the evenings, cane in hand. The young folks of the parish sat on the stone wall next to the church on Madison Street waiting to chat with their pastor. Obviously, he was loved by many.

As noted earlier in this history, Saint Mary's School was established in the basement of the first church building in 1850. In October 2, 1887, a new school constructed specifically for education was blessed. Since Bishop Bayley, the first Bishop of Newark, had been devoted to the establishment of parish schools, the new building was eventually to be named for him—the Bayley School. Ten years later, the Bayley School initiated a two-year high school course, concentrating on commercial subjects. In 1904, the Bayley High School was accredited as a secondary school offering a two-year commercial course. In 1908, Bayley High School relocated into the old convent on Madison Street, which had originally served as the first rectory. Father Ellard was eventually to develop a complete four-year high school course at the Bayley High School.

Father Ellard had a strong interest in the Bayley School. During his pastorate, Bayley School continued to grow. When the enrollment reached more than 150, he remodeled what had been the sisters' convent on Madison Street behind the church, then used by the Bayley High School. He also added two new rooms to the Bayley School. In 1923 the high school was formally established as a four-year

Father Ellard on his horse, a common mode of transportation for early Assumption pastors.

8/1937 Parish Review

The Bayley High School, shown here in 1948.

1972 Assumption Custom Book, p.23

The reconstructed All Souls Hospital, mid-20th C. The building is now used as the Atlantic Rehabilitation Institute of the Morristown Medical Center.

Caritas, Sisters of Charity, p.212

high school. Recognizing that Bayley High School was becoming overcrowded, he created a fund for the construction of a new high school, which would one day be named Bayley-Ellard High School. The Bayley-Ellard High School would eventually be constructed in Madison and continue in operation until 2005. He oversaw the construction of the new All Souls Hospital, the nursing residence, and the maternity hospital, which were gifts of Louis Thebaud of Madison. Sadly, the building then being used for the All Souls Hospital, the Arnold Tavern, burned down one month before the opening of the new hospital.

Father Ellard was devoted to the hospital and its patients. It was reported that he visited the hospital every day, making a complete tour and stopping in every room.

To accommodate the needs of the Sisters of Charity, he purchased the Ballantine House at the corner of Macculloch Avenue and Perry Street from Isabel A. Ballantine on June 26, 1916, for the sum of $8,500, converting it into a convent. In the autumn of 1916, twelve Sisters of Charity moved into their new convent. This building is presently used as the Assumption Ministry Center. (See The Convent section of this publication for more details.)

The interior of the church as it appeared in 1915.

1972 Assumption Custom Book, p.21

In the fall of 1918, the world was struck by the "Spanish" influenza pandemic. More than 17,000 residents of New Jersey died in the last three months of 1918 from this disease. When the Grey Nuns were bedridden at All Souls Hospital, the Sisters of Charity of Bayley School volunteered in shifts to take their place.

Parish societies continued to flourish at Assumption during Father Ellard's pastorate. A parade of the Holy Name Society along South Street was started around 1919 and continued into the 1970s, always on the second Sunday of October. Also in 1919, the Knights of Columbus acquired the Young Men's Catholic Association Building on South Street.

Father Ellard was named a monsignor by Pope Pius XI at the request of Bishop Walsh, and on October 19, 1929, he was vested with the robe of his office. He was subsequently named the Dean of Morris and Sussex Counties.

At the request of Monsignor Ellard, Saint Margaret Church, which had been functioning as a mission of Assumption, was made a separate parish in 1930. At that time, it was unofficially estimated that there were 2,900 members at Assumption and 2,100 at Saint Margaret's.

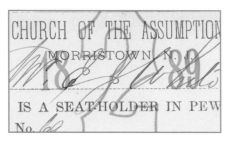

Pew Ticket.
From the Personal Collection of Mary Louise Hallinan Smith, parishioner

Monsignor Ellard was responsible for installing a plaque memorializing the men of Assumption who served their country during the Great War (World War I). The plaque can be seen to this day on the left side of the Maple Avenue entrance to the church. Three hundred twenty-eight of our men served, with seven making the supreme sacrifice.

A 1937 issue of *The Parish Review* reported that the largest Sunday contribution for the month of August was five dollars given by Mr. and Mrs. Eugene Burke. Most of the reported contributions were in the one- to two-dollar range.

Monsignor Ellard died on Sunday, August 15, 1937, the Feast of the Assumption of the Blessed Virgin Mary which, of course, is also the feast day for which our parish is named. Monsignor Ellard was sixty-five and had been a priest for forty years. More than 1,000 people jammed into the church for his funeral Mass. Extra chairs were put into the side aisles, and many were standing in the rear. Nonetheless, all who wished could not gain access into the church; they listened respectfully outside. The Mass was celebrated by the Most Reverend Thomas H. McLaughlin, Auxiliary Bishop of Newark. The local media reported that at the time of his death there were 5,000 Catholics in Morristown, and Assumption was referred to "as the largest local church" (*Parish Review,* August 1937, pp.10-11).

Monsignor Ellard was succeeded by Father Edward J. Barrett on December 16, 1937. Father Barrett was born on September 1, 1881, and ordained in 1910. He had served in Sacred Heart Church in Newark for sixteen years. Father Barrett saw to the maintenance of the parish plant. In those days, Assumption Church was ivy-covered. During his pastorate, the bricks of the church were repointed and the rectory and convent remodeled. Rents were still being charged for the pews in the church. Indeed, during this period turnstiles were installed at the entrance, and a parishioner would put money into the turnstile to obtain a pew ticket!

The societies and sodalities of the parish continued in operation. The Rosary Society and the Holy Angels met on the first Sunday of the month, the senior and junior Holy Name Societies on the second Sunday, and the Children of Mary on the third Sunday. A perpetual novena in honor of Our Lady of the Miraculous Medal was held every Monday evening at 8:00 p.m. The Guard of Honor, which remains active to this day and is, perhaps, better known as the Ushers, was established on Sunday, January 5, 1941. They met on the first Monday of each month, following the novena. In those days, the Guard of Honor was open only to men of the parish. The work of the Guard of Honor was, primarily, to maintain order in the church!

The redecorated interior of the church in 1948.

*100th Anniversary of the
Church of the BVM, p.12*

On June 7, 1949, the property of Judge Parker at 63 Macculloch Avenue was purchased by the Church of the Assumption for $31,500. This was to become the future home of Assumption School. Interestingly, there was a restriction put into the contract which stated that no school was to be built on the property for a period of five years. This resulted from neighborhood opposition to the sale of the property.

In 1948, the parish celebrated the 100th anniversary of the founding of the Church of the Assumption of the Blessed Virgin Mary. To commemorate this event, the church was redecorated and refurbished. The small organ, which formerly had been in the sanctuary for the use of the chancel choir, was removed. In its place a beautiful new altar of white Carrera marble, duplicating Our Lady's altar, was erected. A white marble statue of Saint Joseph, made possible through the generosity of two Morristown sisters, Margaret and Susan Hawes, was placed over the altar. The sanctuary was enlarged, and a new terrazzo marble floor replaced the red carpet. The large pulpit was removed and a new, small, hand-wrought iron pulpit was placed in the sanctuary to facilitate preaching. A Western Electric amplifying system was installed. The inadequate lighting fixtures were removed and new, concealed lights replaced them, providing improved illumination in the sanctuary and the body of the church (Miekam, p.15).

Thanks in part to bequests to Assumption from the estates of Margaret and Susan Hawes, the Diocese of Paterson purchased the Walker estate in Madison in 1948, which later became the site of Bayley-Ellard High School. The property consisted of a 35-room mansion, carriage house, swimming pool, and squash court. The contract between the church and Parthenia B. Walker to buy the property for $150,000 was assigned to the diocese for consummation of the purchase and establishment of the school. The diocese operated the school on the thirty-five-acre site until 2005 when the school closed due to financial and enrollment issues.

As Monsignor Barrett lay on his deathbed, he was heard by those keeping vigil to have recited the following poem/prayer repeatedly:

Afraid, dear Lord? No, not afraid
Of Thy judgment's just decree,
But ashamed, my God, ah yes ashamed
To lift my eyes to Thee.

When the sands of my life are drifting out
And I stand upon death's lone pier,
My heart may sink with an honest shame
But never a thought of fear.

Ashamed that One Whom I dearly love
Who gave me a work to do,
Who coming at eve'n findeth me
To my noble Friend untrue.

But afraid, my God, why should I fear?
You formed and fashioned this clay.
You knew the feeble thing I was
When You gave me the light of day.

The small mean things that are mine to give,
Others' eyes would not deign to see.
Yet You stoop and take with a loving smile
Well knowing 'tis only me.

If I fear Thee, God, I could not go on
So I'll choose the better part.
I'll hide myself and my broken life
In the depths of Thy Sacred Heart.

I will kneel at Thy feet and with head bowed low
In shame at the waste of years,
But hopeful still, or my crucified God
Yet awaiteth my penitent tears.

With life's pages all blurs and blots throughout
I will trust Thee on to the end,
For there waits at the lonely pier of death
My kindest, truest Friend.

—Author Unknown

Illustration of the Assumption School, constructed and located on Macculloch Avenue.

Assumption School Dedication Program, Centerfold

On December 2, 1953, Monsignor Barrett went home to the Lord and was buried in front of the church. He was succeeded by Father Francis Doogan, a pastorate remembered by a few of our current parishioners. Francis J. Doogan was born in Ireland in 1887. He was appointed pastor at Assumption by Bishop McNulty on January 21, 1954.

Father Doogan's greatest accomplishment while pastor at Assumption was the construction of the new Assumption School on Macculloch Avenue. The estate of Judge Parker had been purchased by Assumption in 1949. Monsignor Barrett had hoped to construct a school on this site, but world events—the Depression, World War II, and the Korean Conflict—interfered. Just twenty months and four days after becoming pastor, Father Doogan broke ground for the new school on Sunday afternoon, September 25, 1955. It is fitting that a parish with a long Irish heritage would dedicate its new school on March 17, 1957, with the laying of the cornerstone by Bishop McNulty. Under the direction of Sister Michael Maria and Brother Benedict Meyer, OSB, the children gave a splendid musical performance.

A new school was badly needed at Assumption. The old Bayley School was not particularly well-maintained. Both this building and the Bayley High School

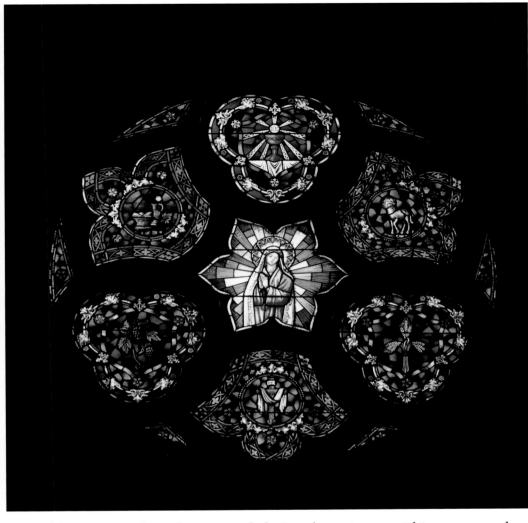

Assumption's Rose Window.
© *Sergio Burani—Photos by Sergio*

were old, repurposed, and overcrowded. One long-time parishioner remembers Father Doogan announcing at Sunday Mass that ground would soon be broken for the new Assumption School. People cried happy tears because it was so badly needed. The old Bayley [Grammar] School and High School, as well as the old sacristy, were subsequently demolished. A new sacristy was constructed in 1958.

Nocturnal Adoration of the Most Blessed Sacrament was inaugurated on September 1, 1956, for the First Friday of each month. Women were present for adoration during the day, and men took over for the evening hours. Eucharistic Adoration was augmented with the creation of the Eucharistic Guild in 1960. The

Exterior of the church in 1967.

*Hudson Robert Huff, Studio of
Photography, Livingston, New Jersey,
12/06/1967.*

Guild was composed of women and high school girls who took turns spending one-half hour before the Blessed Sacrament on the First Friday of the month. The Guild started with 200 members. Eucharistic Adoration was to continue at least through the 1960s.

The rose window that graces the Maple Avenue side of the church was installed in 1956 by Hiemer and Company of Clifton, New Jersey, with other stained glass windows in the area of the former choir loft.

Father Doogan was a priest of the "old school." He has been described by parishioners who knew him as being "unique" and "somewhat of a character." He was very much involved with the myriad details of the parish, especially with Assumption School. He believed in micromanaging the school. If a parish meeting were to be held in the school on a given morning, the keys to the school were not given out until the morning of the meeting. The person in charge of the meeting would go to the rectory at 6:00 a.m. to obtain the keys to the building to obtain access.

Father Doogan's hobby was traveling. He went to Ireland a number of times, to the Holy Land, and around the world.

During Father Doogan's later years, the physical plant deteriorated. The church was dark and dreary. Holy Rood Cemetery was not well-maintained. The grass was not cut, and it became overgrown. Obviously, new leadership was required.

Because of illness, Father Doogan, who had celebrated the golden jubilee of his ordination in 1964, resigned as pastor on August 23, 1966, and was named pastor emeritus. Father John Dericks was named as pastor. Father Doogan continued to reside at Assumption until his death in 1968. As with Monsignor Barrett, Father Doogan was buried in front of the church he had served.

Father Dericks immediately set about the work of redecorating the church. In the summer of 1968, as a result of an anonymous contribution, the church was repainted, and the former dark and dreary look was replaced with a bright, freshly painted surface.

However, the financial condition of the parish was troubling, one factor being the creation of the parish of Saint Thomas More in the Convent Station section of Morris Township. In 1966, it was estimated that 500 Catholic families lived in that area, which was part of the territory of the Church of the Assumption. In those

Bingo! Typical Saturday afternoon at Assumption School in the early 1970s.
1972 Assumption Custom Book, p.15

days, there was considerable friction between Morristown and Morris Township. This had developed as a result of the Morristown Board of Education on October 17, 1955, notifying Township residents that within three years Township students would no longer be accepted at Morristown High School due to overcrowding. This set off sixteen years of feuding between the Town and the Township, which was not settled until June 29, 1971, when the New Jersey State Supreme Court ruled that the Town and the Township constituted one community and that the Morristown and Morris Township school districts must be merged into one. As a result, the Morris School District, comprising the Town and the Township, was created, and has been an enormous success.

However, in 1966, the feelings on the part of the Convent Station residents were running high. After the creation of the new parish in 1966 and until the construction of Saint Thomas More in 1969, the Convent Station residents attended Mass at Holy Family Chapel on the campus of the College of Saint Elizabeth rather than attending in Morristown. As a result, the weekly collections at Assumption plummeted, at times reaching a low of $1,500. Something had to be done to augment parish finances, which showed a deficit of $58,373 in 1967. Emergency collections were instituted on each Sunday. To further increase parish income, bingo was established in 1972, taking place in the school gymnasium on Tuesday evenings and on Saturdays. Most of those playing bingo were not parishioners. On a day when bingo cleared $1,000, a bottle of champagne was opened and made available to the hard-working bingo volunteers. To further augment parish finances, a car raffle was instituted in 1968, and newspaper and aluminum were collected for recycling; the parish was paid a fee for these materials. A parish carnival was initiated but had to be terminated because of vandalism. It is difficult for us today to fully appreciate how bad the financial condition of the parish was. Today Assumption is one of the wealthiest parishes in the diocese. In the late Sixties and through the Seventies, the parish struggled. Indeed, a 1972 publication entitled *The Church of the Assumption* referred to the parish as being "impoverished."

Over the preceding twenty years, there had been a gradual phasing out of societies and sodalities at Assumption. In the late 1960s, there was still mention in parish publications of the Holy Name Society, Apostleship of Prayer, and the Legion of Mary. As the Seventies advanced, mention was no longer made of these organizations. However the Rosary Society would continue to be active in the parish at least through the Seventies. The Women of Assumption, composed of all the women in the parish, was active in 1968 and continued to meet through the Seventies. The Friendship Club, composed of Assumption seniors and the forerunner of today's Assumption Seniors, was also established in the Seventies. The counterpart of the Women of Assumption, the Assumption Men's Group— primarily a social club—was also active during the Seventies.

One of the organizations created by Father Dericks that was to have a significant role during his pastorate was the Parish Council, established in 1967. Elections to the Parish Council were held on an annual basis with all parishioners given the opportunity to vote.

One of the proposals that the Parish Council was asked to consider was the disposition of the property on the corner of Madison Street and Macculloch Avenue, now referred to as the lower parking lot. The area in question is part of the "Little Dublin" section of Morristown. During the Dericks pastorate, a number of small houses that lined Madison Street and Macculloch Avenue were acquired by the church and demolished. This included "The Beehive," a multi-family residential structure that had become run down. It had been acquired by Cornelius Holly in 1890 and moved to this location. It is quite likely that "The Beehive" was the original Assumption Church building that had been sold by the church and moved to the Madison Street/Macculloch Avenue location. A photograph of "The Beehive" shows little resemblance to the original church building. It was obviously

"The Beehive," circa 1968.

From the collection of the
North Jersey History Center,
Morristown & Morris Township Library

substantially altered to accommodate tenants. "The Beehive" was acquired by the church for $30,000 in October 1967 and demolished. The question was, What should we do with the now-vacant property? Father Dericks, working with a developer, proposed a nine-story building that would be constructed on the empty lot and on the property now containing the Assumption Ministry Center (formerly one of our convents). This proposal caused considerable dissension, both within the Parish Council and among the residents of the affluent Miller Road neighborhood. The developer opted out of the project when he learned that the building would be constructed in a National Register Historic District, which would have made the approvals extremely difficult to obtain. The Parish Council voted to kill the project in August 1976. Subsequently, the former convent was converted into housing for the elderly and named the Dericks Residence. The building is now used as the Assumption Ministry Center.

Because of the serious financial situation in the parish in the late Sixties and well into the Seventies, mention was made on several occasions in the church bulletin that our historic church "…would have to come down!" and a new church constructed. It is difficult to understand this logic. It costs a great deal of money to demolish a building, and certainly the cost of a new church would not be inconsiderable. Nevertheless, and for several years thereafter, such a statement continued to appear in the parish bulletins. Also mentioned in the parish bulletin was the difficulty in maintaining Assumption School. In 1967, kindergarten was discontinued although it was reinstated a few years later. To offset the costs of running the school, some of the classrooms in the school were rented out to the Morristown School District. Enrollment in Assumption School in 1967 was 595; in 1970, 344; and in 1973, it reached a low of 207. In 1971, serious consideration was being given to merging Assumption School with Saint Margaret's School. A non-binding vote was taken within the parish as to the desirability of keeping the school open. The vote was close but in favor of maintaining a parish school. The situation began to turn around when in 1973 Sister June Morrissey, SC, was named principal. An Assumption School golf tournament and fund raiser were inaugurated in 1978. By that time enrollment in the school was on the increase. Today Assumption School, the second oldest continuously operating Catholic school in New Jersey, is an enormous success with 515 students (enrolled in the 2010-2011 school year) from pre-kindergarten to grade 8. The school is considered to be academically excellent and is totally self-sustaining. Much of the credit must go to Sister June; to Sister Merris Larkin, SC, the current principal; to the faculty and staff at the school; and to the extremely supportive parents of the children attending the school.

Because of the liturgical changes that came about as a result of Vatican II, Father Dericks was of the opinion that the old marble altar at the back of the sanctuary was no longer appropriate. Starting around 1972, he had placed a gold-colored curtain in front of the altar, hiding it from the view of the congregation. In 1978, based on liturgical practice that dictated only one altar should be in the sanctuary and with a smaller altar already installed in the sanctuary, he announced

Our current altar.
© Sergio Burani—Photos by Sergio

that the old altar would have to be removed. This caused an uproar in the parish. In 1978, there were still a fair number of Assumption parishioners who had been born in Ireland and had come to Morristown with their parents. Many of their parents had "paid for" the altar with their nickels and dimes. A petition was circulated in the parish to block the removal of the altar. The Parish Council considered the question and, by a vote of eight to seven, approved its removal. In June 1978, the altar was removed and cut up. For years after, many parishioners harbored ill feelings about the loss of what they considered to be part of the church's patrimony.

The current altar in our sanctuary is made up of four marble panels from three older altars. One panel is from the former "Our Lady's" altar, and one panel is from the old "St Joseph's" altar. The front and back panels of our present altar are from the original "high" altar of the 1880s. These former altars were mostly made of plaster of paris, painted to resemble marble, and those parts were buried. As noted above, the four marble panels were saved to construct our present main altar.

In 1972, there were other extensive renovations of the sanctuary resulting from some of the changes instituted by Vatican II. The old altar rail was removed as was the altar of the Blessed Virgin Mary. A new tabernacle of a contemporary design representing the ark of the covenant was installed in the former chapel of Our Lady to the left of the sanctuary. The statue of Saint Joseph, located on the right side of the sanctuary, was removed, and in its place a new baptistry was installed. In the baptistry, a bronze dove was suspended from the ceiling.

In 1974, Vincenzo Mussner, a sculptor from Ortisei, Italy, was commissioned to carve a wooden Pieta to replace the statue of the Pieta donated by Mrs. Patrick Welsh in 1887. It is made of linden wood, shaded and waxed, and is now located in the alcove of the Madison Street entrance.

In order to keep the parishioners informed about the happenings in the parish, a publication *The Parish Voice* was published monthly starting in 1968. It was succeeded by *The Tent* in 1976, which was published for a few years.

As mentioned above, during the years of Father Doogan's pastorate, the Holy Rood cemetery was not well maintained. Uncut grass gave the cemetery an unkempt appearance. In 1966, Father Dericks called for volunteers to help clean up and maintain the cemetery. In 1967, he appointed a board of directors for the cemetery. Perpetual care was instituted in 1968. In the 1970s, a large bequest was made to the church for the maintenance of the cemetery. This helped greatly in improving its appearance. By 1974, the cemetery was considered to be "self-supporting." In 1976, the first of what is now four mausoleums was constructed at Holy Rood. Tony DiLorenzo, a parishioner and subsequently a deacon, was appointed by Father Dericks as the manager of Holy Rood Cemetery. He was succeeded by Diane Loughman in 2005 who continues in this capacity. Today, Holy Rood is a well-maintained place of rest for our deceased parishioners and others and is a credit to the parish. (See The Cemetery section of this publication.)

Music has been a central part of Assumption's worship. Some of the finest

Sound of Music performance in the school gym.
1972 Assumption Custom Book, p.15

musicians have directed the choirs and led the people during the liturgical services of the 163 years that this community has been in existence. The parishioners have generously served their parish as choir members.

On November 30, 1954, a new organ, manufactured by the Peragallo Pipe Organ Company of Paterson, New Jersey, was purchased and installed at a cost of almost $20,000. This replaced the previous organ, which had seen long and honorable service for almost seventy years. The Peragallo organ was to remain in use until destroyed in the disastrous fire of April 10, 1985. The Peragallo organ was replaced in 1986 by an organ manufactured by Gress-Miles. It is a three-manual organ with forty-six ranks and 2,486 pipes. It is one of the noteworthy organs in Morristown. The organ was designed by then Music Director/organist Marc McGinnis and is tonally French in style. It was built and installed by Ed Gress of the Gress-Miles Organ Company of Princeton, New Jersey, and was played for the first time at the Triduum of 1987. The present beautifully handcrafted console was built and designed by John Peragallo III, grandson of John Peragallo, Sr., who installed the 1954 organ. The third generation of the Peragallo Organ Company of Paterson, New Jersey, still cares for and maintains the Assumption Church organ. During the renovation of 2007 the console was installed on the main floor of the church by John Peragallo III.

From records in the archives of the Diocese of Paterson, we know that Honore Ginty was organist and choir director at Assumption for three years during the early Fifties. She directed both the adult and children's choir. When Father Dericks became pastor in 1966, Joan Meitzler was the organist. Mrs. Meitzler continued in this capacity until 1974 and was followed by Kevin Norris as music director, organist, and published composer of liturgical music. Church music by the great church composers was performed by the choir at the Sunday noon Mass and was listed in the newly issued church bulletin. This music was supplemented by guest artists who performed during Mass. Because of the precarious financial condition of the parish, these artists' performances were financed through contributions from individual choir members. Because of illness, Mr. Norris was forced to step down as minister of music in 1985. He was succeeded by Marc Anthony McGinnis, who continued to emphasize high-quality church music. Mr. McGinnis was in turn succeeded by Claudia Nardi on October 1, 1986, who continues in the capacity of director of music ministry today, twenty-five years later.

Ms. Nardi plans and coordinates the parish liturgical program and conducts the children, youth, and adult choirs as well as the women's schola. She has also served as director and coordinator for many diocesan cathedral liturgies and larger choirs, including Bishop Rodimer's Fiftieth Anniversary Mass. Serving with Ms. Nardi from 1993-2008 was organist Liz Mancinelli. She was succeeded by Karen Chiappini, our current organist who has twenty-five years of experience in the field and, like those before her, continues the fine tradition of artistry and liturgy in service to Assumption Church.

One of the delightful and highly successful innovations during the Dericks pastorate was the Assumption Theater. Created and led by Terry Koyce, the Assumption Theater annually performed well-known Broadway shows in the gymnasium of Assumption School. Its first production was *The Sound of Music* followed in 1973 with *Fiddler on the Roof*. Subsequent performances given annually included *George M!*, *South Pacific*, *Foot Light Follies*, *Annie Get Your Gun*, *Foot*

1985 fire that almost destroyed our historic church.

We Remember, We Celebrate, We Believe, p.7

Light Follies II, Show Boat, Guys and Dolls, Camelot, and for the tenth anniversary, *Oklahoma.* These were delightful performances, enjoyed by many. They also provided another source of revenue for a still-struggling parish.

As a result of Vatican II, the permanent diaconate was established in the Catholic Church. On June 8, 1974, Assumption's first deacon, Gabriel (Gabe) Lasch, was ordained at the Cathedral of Saint John the Baptist in Paterson. An inspiration to all, he was to serve as a deacon until his death on June 24, 2003. Deacon Lasch's ordination was followed by those of Bill Harty, Tony DiLorenzo, Frank Para, Mike Hanly, Tom Spruiell, Richard Pinto, Jim Butkus, and Brian Beyerl. At one time Assumption had seven active deacons!

On July 7, 1981, Father Dericks was elevated to the dignity of a monsignor.

The financial situation of the parish during the Seventies remained precarious. Indeed as late as 1979, Father Dericks announced that the parish was barely holding its own financially. A special collection on each fifth Sunday of the month was taken to address the financial situation.

However, as we entered the 1980s, the financial condition seemed to improve. Weekly collections increased to about $4,000, up from $2,500 or less during the Seventies.

But on the evening of April 10, 1985, disaster struck! Air conditioning was being installed in the church, and a workman had left on a 1000-watt lamp in the crawl space above the ceiling of the building, which ignited the wood in this area.

A passing motorist on Maple Avenue noticed a fire in the roof of the church and rushed to the rectory to notify the priests who called 911. Father Chris Muldoon and Marc Anthony McGinnis, the minister of music, rushed into the church. Father Muldoon retrieved the Blessed Sacrament from the tabernacle, and Mr. McGinnis tried to remove from the church what he could. The fire fighters arrived promptly, but the fire was far advanced. The roof and much of the walls of the church were completely destroyed. Indeed, experts later commented that, if the destruction of the walls had proceeded by another foot or two, the entire church would have been lost. As it was, it would take a year and one-half to restore this magnificent building to its former splendor, but restored it would be. After eighteen months of Masses in the school gymnasium, Midnight Mass was celebrated in the church on Christmas Eve, 1986. The pews had not yet been installed and folding chairs were used, but our magnificent church was back in operation. The joy of the congregation that evening knew no bounds! (See Father Christopher Muldoon's recollection of this event in the Reminiscences section of this publication.)

Monsignor Dericks retired in 1986 after twenty years as our pastor. He was replaced by Monsignor Michael Conway as our fourteenth pastor on September 12, 1986.

Monsignor Conway's tenure as pastor at Assumption would prove to be short. During his three and one-half years as our shepherd, he endeared himself to many by his deep spirituality and his brilliant homilies. However, this was offset by considerable friction between the pastor and Assumption School.

In February 1987, Monsignor Conway announced that the parish was free of debt and had a small surplus. However, the subsidy to the school at this time was $138,000 or 27 percent of the school budget. In the ensuing three years, considerable friction developed between the pastor and the school, no doubt resulting from what Monsignor Conway perceived to be the drain on parish finances resulting from the operation of the school. Counterbalancing this was the strong support of the school and its principal by the parents of the children enrolled there.

Monsignor Conway put an end to bingo and the car raffle, no doubt to the relief of many in the parish. Weekly collections had increased somewhat, being in the neighborhood of $6,500 to $7,000 on a given weekend. Newspapers were still collected and sold.

The Rosary Society and the Women of Assumption remained active. These organizations were supplemented by ministries to the divorced and separated and the Joshua Discussion Group. Antioch, a weekend for teens led by teens with the assistance of a priest, was initiated in 1991. The Dericks Residence, the site of the former convent of the Sisters of Charity and now the Assumption Ministry Center, was in operation as a residence for seniors.

Monsignor Conway resigned as pastor of Assumption and in January of 1990 was appointed administrator of Saint Simon the Apostle Church in Green Pond. Father James Canosa was appointed administrator of Assumption effective January 8, 1990. After assuming that position, Father Canosa announced to a shocked congregation that the parish was "broke." Obviously, Assumption was in need of a period of healing. This was to be provided by a Morristown native who was appointed pastor on February 12, 1990—Monsignor Martin F. Rauscher.

Upon assuming the responsibilities as pastor of Assumption Parish, Monsignor Rauscher set about putting the affairs of the parish in order. He discovered that many parents were not paying the tuition for their children who were enrolled in the school. He conducted a phone-a-thon to raise money for the school and the parish. The phone-a-thon raised $101,325 for the school and $69,612 for the church. The total parish debt was $291,148, and the annual deficit was estimated to be $143,960. The fund drive more than made up for the annual deficit. In addition, tuition in the school was raised by twenty-five percent. A fund-raising dinner dance was initiated to supplement parish income.

Monsignor Rauscher met with Sister June Morrissey, SC, the principal at Assumption School, and established an excellent working relationship with her. In those days, the parish was fortunate to still have a substantial number of faculty provided by the Sisters of Charity of Saint Elizabeth. Present on the teaching staff, in addition to Sister June, were Sisters Merris Larkin (currently the school principal), Gertrude Fitzsimmons and Beverly Ornes. Also teaching at the school at this time was Sister Marie Graziano.

Sister Patricia Marks was hired as director of religious education on July 15, 1990. Sister Marks was to serve in this capacity and in the Good Shepherd program until her retirement in 2007.

The Women of Assumption, the Joshua Group, Adult Enrichment, the Ministry to Separated and Divorced Catholics, and the Rosary Society continued to be active.

All things considered, it was an excellent beginning to what was to become a pastorate of accomplishment, which was to continue for almost twenty years.

In 1991, Sister Pat Godri, SC, was hired as a pastoral associate. She was to become an integral part of Assumption in the four years she was to remain with us.

One of the hallmarks of the Rauscher years was the outreach of the parish to the poor. In 1992, Monsignor Rauscher announced that fourteen percent of the parish's gross of $700,000, or $100,000, was given to various organizations that served the needs of the less fortunate in Morris County and beyond.

The financial situation of the parish began to improve. Tuition at Assumption School was raised twice in a two-year period. This, in addition to increased church revenues, led to a decrease in the parish debt of $47,465 over two years.

A ministerial council had been formed in 1991 to advise Monsignor

The Parish Center.
Assumption Parish Files

Rauscher on matters pertaining to spirituality, education, and social activities and outreach. In addition to the Rosary Society and the Legion of Mary (the only two societies still active in the parish), ministries were initiated in Christian Service, the Food Pantry, the Interfaith Council of the Homeless, Habitat for Humanity, and the Soup Kitchen. Indeed during the Rauscher years the types of societies that once dominated the life of the parish would eventually disappear, replaced by various ministries oriented toward the young, the old, and those buffeted by the vicissitudes of life. Examples of the last are the Bereavement Group, supporting those who have lost a loved one, and the Ministry to the Divorced and Separated. The Women of Assumption continued to be active. It is interesting to note that twenty years later many of these ministries continue to function at Assumption. (See The Ministry Center section of this publication.)

In 1993, Monsignor Rauscher announced that because of the increased activity in the parish there was a need for a substantial meeting space. He proposed a fund drive to construct a parish center to be built at the rear of the church. A drive eventually resulted in contributions of $627,000. The parish center was constructed using plans developed by the architectural firm of Daniel Krief Associates of New York City, completed in 1994 and blessed on October 15 of the same year.

Parish finances continued to show some improvement. However, the operation of Assumption School continued to be subsidized by the parish in the amount of $159,000. In 1994, Sister June Morrissey, principal of Assumption School, was named "Educator of the Year" by the Sisters of Charity. Sister June was to resign as principal of Assumption School in 1995. She was succeeded as principal by Sister Merris Larkin, SC, who remains as principal to this day.

Monsignor Rauscher reported that in 1994, senior citizens composed twenty-five percent of the parish community.

A ministry to the deaf was initiated in 1997 and continues to this day. Pews are reserved for the hearing-impaired at one of the Sunday Masses, which is signed by a professional American Sign interpreter. Many hearing-impaired Catholics from northern New Jersey have been served at Assumption throughout the years.

During 1998, the financial situation showed additional improvement, with the reduction of the parish debt to $100,000. An anonymous contribution of $100,000 from a parishioner greatly abetted this accomplishment.

The year 1999 saw the last mention of the two remaining societies at Assumption: the Rosary Society and the Legion of Mary. In an earlier period, societies and sodalities were a vital part of Assumption parish. However, as noted above, with the passage of time the orientation of the parish changed, with ministries coming to the fore. Indeed, as of the writing of this history, Assumption is blessed with thirty-five works and ministries involving all age groups and types of parish activities—liturgical, social, and outreach. (See the Ministry Center section for the current list.)

In 2000, the Diocese of Paterson initiated the "Prepare the Way" campaign. Assumption's goal was $745,000. An indication of the improvement in the financial health of the parish was the fact that $1,572,041 was contributed by Assumption parishioners, double the amount of the parish goal.

The year 2000 also saw the initiation of a new ministry, Holistic Health, led by Carole Hires, RN, and Michelle Cameron, RN. This ministry is concerned with the physical well-being of Assumption parishioners. Blood pressure screening following Mass became common, continuing to this day.

Outreach to the poor continued to be a vital part of life at Assumption. In 2001, the parish gave $213,816 to various charities in New Jersey and elsewhere.

One of the parish's icons retired in 2001. After twenty-five years in residence at Assumption, celebrating Mass daily and ministering to the elderly in nursing homes and to the sick at Morristown Memorial Hospital where he was a Catholic chaplain, Monsignor William Glennon retired. Monsignor Glennon, who had lived at the rectory at Assumption for those twenty-five years, moved to the Franciscan Retirement Center in Denville where he lived until his death on November 23, 2003. Having served so long at Assumption, he was greatly loved.

The Good Shepherd Catechesis was founded in 2002. This was a program that applies Montessori principles to religious education for children ages three to six. Assumption's program was founded by Sister Pat Marks and Sister Marie Graziano. This ministry was certified by the International Good Shepherd Organization and continues to this day. Also initiated in 2002 was the Centering Prayer group, a contemplative approach to prayer.

The Golden Honor Roll was established in 2002. This was intended to honor Assumption parishioners who had made significant contributions to the parish over a number of years. The initial honorees were Deacon Gabe Lasch, Dave and Irene Phelan, Bill and Claire Harty, Sister Gertrude Fitzsimmons, and Joycelyn Rigassio. The complete listing of the Golden Honor Roll is given in The Ministry Center Section of this publication.

Also in 2005, the parish acquired what is now the Assumption Ministry Center from the Dericks House Corporation. This is the building acquired by the church in 1916 from the Ballantine estate during the period of Morristown's Gilded Age and used for many years as a convent for the Sisters of Charity teaching at Assumption School. For a few years in the 1970s, it was known as the Dericks Residence, providing housing for senior citizens. The Dericks House Corporation had acquired the building from the Church of the Assumption. To make the building suitable for senior housing, the corporation had obtained a $500,000 mortgage from the Diocese. The Corporation had difficulty making payments on this loan. At this point, the parish stepped in and offered the diocese $150,000 for the building, and the diocese forgave the remaining $350,000 due on the note. As a result, the parish once again took possession of the building, which is now being successfully used as the Assumption Ministry Center, housing a number of parish outreach activities.

The Interior of Assumption (March 2011), when viewed through a fisheye lens, resembles "The Barque of Peter"—a symbol of the Church.

© Sergio Burani—Photos by Sergio

Assumption's Sanctuary, Easter 2011.

© Sergio Burani—Photos by Sergio

In 2006, the fourth of our mausoleums was constructed at Holy Rood Cemetery. These mausoleums provide an attractive alternative to in-ground interment for one's loved ones. They also provide meditation areas and chapels for those wishing to pray for and remember their deceased.

The year 2007 saw the retirement of Sister Pat Marks and Sister Marie Graziano. These two sisters, greatly loved by the Assumption community, became parishioners at Assumption in 1978. Sister Graziano had taught religion at Assumption School from 1980 to 1995 and then joined Sister Pat in the Religious Education program. For many years Sister Pat wrote a column in the parish bulletin.

The Dolores Hulvat Catechetical Award was established in 1997. This award memorializes the life and work of Assumption parishioner Dolores Hulvat who for many years served at Assumption in Religious Education and Catechesis until her death in 1997 at the age of fifty-nine. A list of all recipients of this award appears in the Ministry Center section of this publication.

Early in 2007, Monsignor Rauscher advised the parish that the interior of the church was in need of renovation. He contacted the architectural firm of Daniel Krief Associates to develop a plan for the interior of the church in keeping with the architecture of the church. The renovation commenced in April of 2007 and was completed the following September. The cost was approximately $1,800,000 which was contributed by the parishioners.

When Monsignor Rauscher celebrated his seventy-fifth birthday, he was required by church policy to submit his resignation as pastor to the bishop. Bishop Arthur Serratelli asked him to remain temporarily in that role, which he did. However, on September 8, 2009, he officially retired after nineteen and one-half years of devoted service. He was succeeded by Assumption's sixteenth pastor, Monsignor John E. Hart.

Monsignor John E. Hart is a native of Brooklyn. His family moved to Clifton, New Jersey, when John was eleven years old. Monsignor Hart is a graduate of Seton Hall University, where he majored in French. He also holds a Master of Arts degree in Theology with a concentration in Sacred Scripture from Immaculate Conception Seminary, Darlington, New Jersey, and a Licentiate in Canon Law from Saint Paul University, Ottawa, Canada. Monsignor Hart was elevated to the dignity of a monsignor on August 14, 2003.

In the two years that Monsignor Hart has been our pastor, we can already see

Our new crucifix, installed on April 15, 2011, in time for Holy Week, graces the sanctuary directly over the altar.

© Sergio Burani—Photos by Sergio

the impact of his leadership. Assumption is now a tithing parish with parishioners asked to contribute one-tenth of their take-home pay to religious and charitable activities. One half, or five percent, of this amount would go to the church. This has already had a marked impact on parish finances.

One of the challenges that developed shortly after Monsignor Hart's arrival was the condition of the church's steeple. Being 139 years old, our historic church requires constant attention. During the summer of 2011, it was discovered that significant remedial work was required on the church steeple. The repairs of old buildings are not inexpensive. The cost is estimated to be $196,700. The repair is scheduled to be completed October of 2011.

Another of Monsignor Hart's innovations is a magnificent crucifix with a representation of the Living Christ that now graces the sanctuary. The crucifix was obtained from Baker Liturgical Art, Southington, Connecticut. It consists of a nine-foot cross with a five-foot corpus suspended over the altar. The cross is mahogany and was fabricated in the United States. The corpus was hand-carved in Italy and is made of linden wood. This beautiful piece was paid for from the balance in the church renovation fund.

We are confident that under Monsignor Hart's leadership, Assumption will continue and, indeed, expand on its long legacy of ministering to the People of God in Morristown.

As we conclude this latest chapter in the history of our great parish, it is inspiring to realize how far the parish has come in the last forty years. In the early 1970s we were struggling to make ends meet. There was serious consideration given to closing our parish school or at least merging it with Saint Margaret's School. Bingo, paper drives, special collections, and other fund raisers were being conducted to help pay the bills. Today, Assumption is a parish community of 2,740 families. It is vibrant and financially secure, indeed one of the wealthiest parishes in the diocese with an outstanding school and religious education program. We have a strong and respected presence in the Morristown community and the Diocese of Paterson. These changes did not just happen. There has been much hard work and dedication from our clergy, school principals, and the thousands of parishioners who have worshipped within the walls of our church during those many years. We are indeed blessed by Almighty God.

the
SCHOOL

Dedicated to

- *the generations of children who attended Assumption School in its many iterations and*

- *the Sisters of Charity and lay teachers who helped imbue them with the knowledge and moral values to live God-directed, successful lives.*

Assumption School, Early Spring 2011.

© Sergio Burani—Photos by Sergio

One wonders what Father McQuaid would think if he could see Assumption School today: a vibrant, excellent elementary educational institution with more than 515 happy youngsters taught by a dedicated faculty. The seeds that he planted in 1850 indeed have borne much fruit.

Father Bernard McQuaid built our first church in 1848. Two years later, he established what was then known as Saint Mary's School in the basement of the church. Twenty-five young scholars composed the student body. It is interesting to note that Father McQuaid established the principle that the school was not of lesser importance than the church. Father McQuaid was supported by his bishop, James Roosevelt Bayley, who believed that "a parish without a school is not worthy of the name."

Mr. Tracey of New York was the first teacher in the school. Mr. Tracey adhered to the principle, "Spare the rod and spoil the child" (Flynn, *Story of a Parish*, p.47). Mr. Tracey was succeeded by Mr. Donlin. Miss Slater of Massachusetts and a Mr. Faulkner taught for a brief period of time before 1860. Miss Maggie O'Brien was subsequently employed, with Miss Robins joining her. Miss Susan Coxe succeeded Miss Robbins. A few years later the teaching staff consisted of Mr. Coyle for the boys and the Misses Coxe and O'Brien for the girls.

The school was a far cry from what we expect to find in today's school buildings. The rooms were dark, very warm in the summer and correspondingly cold in the winter. A great stove for heat stood in the middle of the room with the stovepipe venting through one of the windows. Nevertheless, we have to believe that our young students learned their ABC's in spite of their inelegant surroundings.

The Bayley School
(Saint Mary's Parish School),
pre-1892.

1972 Assumption
Custom Book, p.19

In 1865, the school was found inadequate for the accommodation of the growing number of children and was enlarged at a cost of $800.

In 1872 our present church was constructed during the pastorate of Father James Sheeran. The old church was then altered to accommodate the school children. In 1875, the Sisters of Charity of Saint Elizabeth were invited to assume the teaching duties at Saint Mary's School. This happy arrangement continues to this very day with Sister Merris Larkin, SC, as the principal of Assumption School.

Two sisters commuted from the motherhouse in Convent Station each day. A small room was added to the school and fitted with a stove and cupboard. It was here that the sisters took their lunch.

Shortly before his death, Mr. Thomas Burns donated his house in front of the church, at the northwest corner of Maple Avenue and Madison Street, to Assumption's then-pastor Father Joseph Flynn, who in turn deeded the house and property to the church. The house was altered and furnished, and in January 1882, Sister Gaudentia, SC, as sister servant and Sisters Cecilia Rose, Eugenia, and Teresita took up residence. This convent greatly facilitated the work of the sisters at Saint Mary's School.

As time went on, it became apparent that the old school was no longer adequate. Indeed there was concern about the health of the children in the cramped school. On March 29, 1886, Father Flynn announced his intention to build a new school in the location of the old cemetery at what is now the upper parking lot behind the church. The remains in the old cemetery were disinterred and reburied at Holy Rood. On November 25, 1886, Bishop Winand Wigger of Newark laid the cornerstone of what was to become the Bayley School. Bishop McQuaid, a former Assumption pastor and at this time the Bishop of Rochester, spoke at the dedication, declaring his pride at the success achieved by the Catholic parochial schools

Front Page of the Program for the Solemn Blessing of Saint Mary's Parish School, October 2, 1887.
1972 Assumption Custom Book, p.17

The Bayley High School, shown here in 1948.
1972 Assumption Custom Book, p.23

of Madison and Morristown from such humble beginnings. On September 19, 1887, the children took possession of their new school—still referred to at that time as Saint Mary's Parish School. On October 2, 1887, Bishop Wigger of Newark, accompanied by dignitaries from throughout the state, blessed the new school.

In 1890, the original school was sold to Cornelius Holly for $400 and moved to the corner of Madison Street and Macculloch Avenue. For many years, this building was used as a residence in the Little Dublin area and very likely was the structure referred to as "The Beehive," which no longer stands.

In 1897, an advanced commercial department was established, followed by a two-year high school commercial program in 1904. The parish school, now referred to as the Bayley School, was accredited as a secondary school offering a two-year commercial course.

Architect's rendition of
The Assumption School.
*Assumption School Dedication Program,
Centerfold*

In 1908 a portion of the former rectory, located behind the current church on Madison Street and then serving as the convent for the Sisters of Charity, was used to accommodate high school students. This building was subsequently to become The Bayley High School.

On June 26, 1916, Monsignor Edward Ellard, then pastor at Assumption, purchased the Ballantine estate, located on the corner of Perry Street and Macculloch Avenue, from Isabel A. Ballantine for $8,500. The building was converted into a convent for the Sisters of Charity. The former convent was then converted into use for The Bayley High School, which now offered a complete four-year high school curriculum. Two additional rooms were added to the Bayley School in 1923.

The Bayley High School continued to grow, and by 1937 had more than 150 students. It was obvious that the structure was no longer adequate. Monsignor Ellard started a fund for a new high school which was to be called the Bayley-Ellard High School. In 1948, Monsignor Edward Barrett purchased the thirty-five acre Walker estate in Madison for $150,000, and in 1949 the Bayley-Ellard Regional High School was opened.

On June 7, 1949, Father Francis Doogan purchased the estate of Judge Parker

Sisters of Charity Faculty of 1957 assigned to the new Assumption School [standing, left to right]: Srs. Ruth Anne, Michael Maria, Margaret Maria, Mary Roseaire, John Gertrude; [seated, left to right]: Srs. Rose Celeste (principal) and Agnes Bernard.
Assumption School Dedication Program, p.16

on Macculloch Avenue. On that site on March 17, 1957, the new Assumption of the Blessed Virgin Mary School was formally dedicated by Bishop James McNulty with the children's choir, under the direction of Sister Michael Maria and Brother Benedict, OSB, providing the choral music. The final chapter of the original Bayley School and The Bayley High School took place when in 1958 the buildings were demolished and converted into a parking lot.

The cost to build the new elementary school was $848,598. With a registration of 502 students, the principal,—Sister Rose Celeste, SC,—was assisted by six other members of her order and her lay faculty.

As with all schools, interesting experiences lead to memorable stories. During the early years of the new Assumption School, milk was furnished to the kindergarten class. The milkman made his delivery early each morning, leaving the order at the kindergarten door. However, Sister Rose began to notice that several cartons were missing from the case each day, and she decided to stake out the situation. What she found was quite surprising. Shortly after the delivery, a huge shaggy dog came up to the case, pulled out a carton with its mouth, and ran into the woods behind the school, repeating this action several times. The beneficiaries

Sister June Morrissey, SC, who served as Assumption School's principal from 1973 through 1995.
Assumption School Yearbook

Walt Whitman's words of inspiration grace the entrance lobby of Assumption School. (top right)
© Sergio Burani—Photos by Sergio

I AM LARGER, BETTER THAN I THOUGHT; I DID NOT KNOW I HELD SO MUCH GOODNESS

of this heist were unknown (perhaps its pups?), but this dog knew of the importance of calcium!

School enrollment remained steady for a number of years, reaching 595 in 1967. The year 1968 saw the formation of the Home and School Association, which, like the Mothers' Guild, played an important role in the educational and financial well-being of the school. With the advent of the Home and School Association, fathers took an even more active part in the education of their children.

As we entered the Seventies, the financial situation of the parish deteriorated markedly. School enrollment also declined significantly. In 1970, enrollment was 344 and by 1973 it had declined to a low of 207. As detailed elsewhere in this history, there was concern about the future viability of Assumption School. In 1973 Monsignor John Dericks invited Sister June Morrissey, SC, to stabilize the situation. Sister June was to continue as principal through 1995, and to her goes the major credit for saving Assumption School.

Nevertheless, there were some difficulties. During the administration of Monsignor Michael Conway (1986-1990), considerable friction developed between the pastor and the school. With Monsignor Conway's departure and the appointment of Monsignor Martin Rauscher, the relationship between rectory and school brightened considerably. As noted elsewhere in this history, Monsignor Rauscher conducted a phone-a-thon to raise money for both the school and the church. Parishioners who had children in the school were contacted. Tuition was raised twice, and the financial situation was stabilized.

As more people employed by local corporations began moving into Morristown, the number of Assumption's students ballooned, and additional lay teachers were hired to assist with certain subjects. At one time the first grade had seventy-four students, and a lay teacher taught art and math in a second classroom. The young pupils would move between the two rooms to complete their school day. Additional lay teachers were added to the staff.

Sister June mounted on the wall of the school's reception hall Walt Whitman's words that read, "I am larger, better than I thought; I did not know I held so much goodness." This quote encapsulated her philosophy that an important part of a student's education is belief in his or her abilities to grow, to know, and to contribute to the world. The posting continues to grace the lobby.

Sister June resigned in 1995 after a very successful tenure as Assumption School's principal. She was replaced by Sister Merris Larkin, SC, who remains principal to this day.

As of 2011, Assumption School is healthy and highly respected in the community with a student enrollment of 515 energetic boys and girls in grades Pre-Kindergarten through Eight.

Sister Merris Larkin, SC, is the current principal of Assumption School.

Assumption School Yearbook

the
RECTORY

Dedicated to

*the priests who have lived, labored, and died in the
service of God and the people of Assumption.*

Assumption's rectory, built in the High Victorian period of the late 19th Century.

Assumption Parish Files

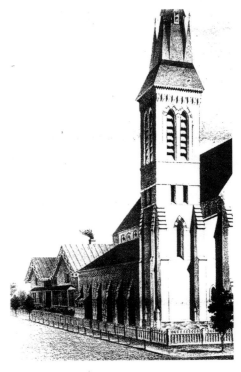

As with Assumption convents, the rectory had at least two different addresses and underwent several renovations in the 163-year history of the parish. The first rectory, to the left of the original church and facing Madison Street, was built and lived in by Father Lawrence Hoey as of 1861. Previous Assumption pastors had lived in Saint Vincent's rectory in Madison or in a Morristown boarding house. This small structure was enlarged in 1880 as the parish grew and associate pastors arrived.

The current rectory, built by Father Joseph Flynn in 1890 and located next to the current church facing Maple Avenue, sits on the site of the original frame church.

Also like the convents, these rectories housed numerous servants of God who worked tirelessly for the parishioners and many others in the community who came to them for consolation, advice, and a helping hand.

As seen in this section of a late 1870s lithograph, our first rectory faced Madison Street and stood at the perimeter of what is now the upper parking lot. Enlarged and remodeled several times before it was torn down in the 1940s, it also served as the second parish convent and the Bayley High School.

G.H.Walker and Company, Boston

The following served Assumption from its inception as an official parish:

Assumption Pastors

Reverend Dominic Senez	1845 – 1848
Reverend Bernard McQuaid	1848 – 1853
Reverend Michael Madden	1853 – 1857
Reverend Lawrence Hoey	1857 – 1867
Reverend James D'Arcy	1867 – 1868
Reverend Patrick McGovern	1868 – 1871
Reverend James Sheeran	1871 – 1881
Rt. Reverend Joseph M. Flynn	1881 – 1910
Reverend George Brown	1910 – 1914
Reverend Edward J. Ellard	1914 – 1937
Rt. Reverend Edward J. Barrett	1937 – 1953
Reverend Francis J. Doogan	1954 – 1966
Monsignor John H. Dericks	1966 – 1986
Monsignor Michael Conway	1986 – 1990
Monsignor Martin F. Rauscher	1990 – 2009
Monsignor John E. Hart	2009 – Present

Throughout its long history, Assumption has been served by numerous curates, associate pastors, or parochial vicars. By any title, they were and continue to be both the right and left arms of the pastors by spearheading many of the duties involved in shepherding a vibrant and growing parish.

1848 – Current
(in the order of their Assumption ministry)

Reverend E. A. Vassallo
Reverend J. M. Girard
Reverend J. Poels
Reverend A. M. Kamme
Reverend I. P. Whelan
Reverend E. Farrell
Reverend J. J. Shannessey

Reverend A. H. Stein
Reverend J. Ginier
Reverend T. M. Donovan
Reverend G DeVincentius
Reverend J. F. Dolan
Reverend C. Clifford
Reverend T. B. Larkin

Reverend J. V. Woods

Reverend T. F. Burke

Reverend F. P. Mestice

Reverend T. A. Mullins

Reverend J. S. Carroll

Reverend J. McCarthy

Reverend B. Marcilla

Reverend J. P. Lenihan

Reverend J. V. Daly

Reverend W. G. Keen

Reverend W. B. Donnelly

Reverend W. A. Looney

Reverend G. S. Stone

Reverend J. P. Smith

Reverend Albert R. Miekam

Reverend James J. Daly

Reverend Leo P. Carey

Reverend J. Francis Feenan

Reverend Daniel A. Vecchiollo

Reverend Michael J. Boland

Reverend Francis X. Dennehy

Reverend John Corr

Reverend John O'Brien

Reverend John H. O'Connor

Reverend Joseph W. Molloy

Reverend Patrick J. Scott

Reverend William W. Lindgren

Reverend Brendan Ryan

Reverend Salvatore A. Campagna

Reverend Allen F. Stepien

Reverend Hubert Maultsby

Reverend William Glennon

Reverend Francis Duffy

Reverend Ray Pavlik

Reverend Gary O'Hare

Reverend Frank Matarazzo

Reverend Bruce Welch

Reverend Christopher Muldoon

Reverend David Mahon

Reverend Joseph McCarthy

Reverend James Canosa

Reverend Joseph Davis

Reverend Mark Olenowski

Reverend William Winston

Reverend Dennis Crowley

Reverend Philip-Michael Tangorra

A number of Assumption's sons have offered their lives in service to God and humankind through the priesthood. The following list has been created from available references at our disposal, but does not include those who entered religious communities.

Assumption Sons Who Have Received Holy Orders as Diocesan Priests

Burke, Monsignor
   Eugene, VF, PA, STD
Carroll, Monsignor Eugene
Casey, Reverend Joseph
Collins, Reverend Leo
Dempsey, Reverend Joseph
Dunn, Monsignor
   William, VF, MR
Duffy, Reverend Thomas
Duffy, Reverend William
Farrelly, Reverend Edward
Hillock, Reverend Edward
Holten, Reverend William
Lasch, Monsignor Kenneth
Lawless, Reverend Christopher

MacDonald, Monsignor James
Mansfield, Reverend Thomas
Marceau, Reverend Paul
McVey, Reverend Paul
Mooney, Reverend William
Moss, Reverend James
Mulhall, Monsignor James
Murray, Monsignor James
O'Neill, Reverend Henry
Rauscher, Monsignor Martin
Rocco, Reverend Remigio
Rutledge, Reverend James
Stokes, Reverend Paul
Sullivan, Reverend Brian
Sullivan, Reverend John

In the 163 years of Assumption's history as an official parish, its two rectories have housed more than seventy dedicated priests, plus scores of visiting seminarians and transitional deacons. Each has had his own story of his road to priesthood. One of the most inspiring and awesome is an episode in the life of our pastor emeritus, Monsignor Martin F. Rauscher, who has related the following vignette several times in homilies and conversations in order to demonstrate that we each have a role to play in God's Great Plan.

When I was a college seminarian at Saint Paul's Abbey in Newton, New Jersey, back in the 1950s, I developed a psychosomatic illness consisting of an upset stomach, sleepless nights, headaches, etc. I sought counsel from a priest at the Abbey, Father Andrew O'Sullivan, to help me deal with my symptoms. He advised me to go to God for healing. I had prayed. Father O'Sullivan asked me why I might be having these symptoms, and I told him I was worried about being unworthy of becoming a priest. Did I have sufficient intelligence? Was I a good enough person? I related to Father O'Sullivan that I was always trying to please others, and all this worrying brought on these symptoms. He said to me that I had to let go and let God worry about how worthy I was or how fit I was to be a priest. He told me that I could not live my life trying to fulfill other people's expectations of me. I had to be myself as God created me and not try to live my life as others would expect.

One day while I was walking in the monastery garden I saw this bright light that enveloped me. I felt peaceful, warm, and loved. After that my symptoms left me for good. I never went back to worrying, and worry has never gotten the best of me since. I thank God always for that.

Looking back, [that experience] has helped me be a better priest in that I know what it is to have psychological problems and illness and how willing God is to help us.

We in the pews can only guess at the stress and pressure of church leadership; and yet our God has provided people willing to dedicate their entire lives to God's work through the Catholic faith. Each of the above-named priests, as well as "interning" future priests, has served and lived among us; and each did his best, within the limitation of his authority and abilities, for Assumption Church and the many souls it has held within its embrace.

the
CONVENT

Dedicated to

the Sisters of Charity,
stalwarts at and of Assumption School.

The third Assumption convent on Macculloch Avenue and Perry Street, circa 1970.

1972 Parish Custom Book, p.14.

As has been covered in other chapters, the Sisters of Charity of Saint Elizabeth assumed responsibility for the education of Assumption's children in January 1875. In the absence of a parish convent, two sisters assigned to what was then known as Saint Mary's School, located in the basement of the original church, commuted each day to and from their motherhouse in what is today known as Convent Station. A small room where they could take their noon break was later added to the little school.

In 1882 Assumption's first parish convent—a house located in front of the church at the northwest corner of Maple Avenue and Madison Street—was established. This structure had been bequeathed by Thomas Burns to the then-pastor, Father Joseph Flynn, who in turn deeded it to the parish to serve as a convent for the growing contingent of five Sisters of Charity then assigned to Assumption's school. After appropriate renovations, Sister Gaudentia, SC, as sister servant, and Sisters Cecilia, Rose, Eugenia, and Teresita moved into their new home in January 1882. As the number of students grew, so did the need for additional sisters, and the little convent had to be further altered, enlarged, and improved in 1885.

When the current rectory was constructed and occupied by the priests of the parish on November 25, 1890, the sisters moved into the old rectory, which met

The second Assumption convent, which had previously served as the first rectory. It later became the Bayley High School.

History of a Parish, p.104

the needs of the expanding teaching staff. This second convent became the Bayley High School in 1908. In June 1916 a large Victorian house located on the corner of Perry Street and Macculloch Avenue was purchased for $8,500 from Isabel A. Ballantine (of the Ballantine brewing family) for the twelve sisters who were then associated with the Bayley Grammar and High Schools. (The number of sisters was reduced to eight after Bayley-Ellard High was opened in 1949.) Currently called the Ministry Center, this property housed Sisters of Charity from 1916 until 1981. The building, with its thirty-two rooms, could accommodate a total number of twenty women; the dining room, with two large refectory tables and as many chairs as needed, was large enough to seat that number at one time.

Kathleen Murphy, SC (Sister Mary Roseaire), who taught first grade and later fifth grade for seventeen years at Assumption, lived for most of that time in that house and delighted in its grace and charm. Due to the great need for sisters to staff schools after World War II, she had begun teaching in 1947 during her first year of novitiate. Her second year as a novice was spent back at the motherhouse

Sister Mary Roseaire (Kathleen Murphy, SC) taught first grade for many years at the new Assumption School.

Caritas, Sisters of Charity, p.200

where she prepared for her temporary vows. Sister Kathleen remembers the full but happy days at Assumption. A sister's typical schedule:

5:15 a.m.	Awaken / Prepare for the day
	Mass / Breakfast / Light housekeeping
	One-half hour of adoration of the Blessed Sacrament
8:30	Arrive in classroom
9:00-Noon	Teach class
12-12:30 p.m.	Lunch at the convent
1:00-3:00	Teach class
3:00-4:00	Grade papers or complete assigned work as sacristan, cook, etc.
4:45	Recitation of the rosary at the convent
5:00-6:00	Dinner
6:00-7:00	Chores
7:00-8:15	Recreation
8:15	Start of the "Great Silence"
	(Silence was maintained from 8:15 p.m. to 8:00 a.m.)

If sisters were still working toward their college degrees, they attended classes on Saturday. All taught Sunday School (today's Religious Education Program).

The sisters not only taught school but were responsible for the upkeep of the convent's thirty-two rooms, done after school or on weekends, including wiping walls and washing and waxing floors to hospital-standard cleanliness. Principal Sister Catherine Gertrude maintained a simple but lovely environment. "It was truly our home, a comfortable home in a gracious old house," Sister Kathleen remembers. "We were blessed to have our own chapel, and, when we could not attend Mass in church during the week, one of the parish priests would celebrate 6:30 Mass in the convent chapel for us. Of course we attended Sunday Mass in the church."

During the Christmas season, a crèche was erected in the chapel, a decorated tree graced the community (living) room, and, as in many other homes in the neighborhood, stockings were hung at the fireplace.

"These were wonderful women who truly cared about the children they taught, and we ourselves treated each other as family. We could not go home for the holidays in those days, so we were indeed each others' family. The elders were my mentors, and the younger were my sisters. What wonderful memories I have of life at Assumption," recalls Sister Kathleen.

From 1976 to 1981, the convent was rented to the Sisters of Charity, who used it as a formation center and novitiate for women joining the order. The four sisters remaining at Assumption had been moved to a smaller house at 8 Perry Street, purchased in December 1973 for $59,000. In 1981, with only one sister (Principal June Morrissey) residing in the convent, the 8 Perry Street house was renovated. Sister June moved to the third floor and a lay couple rented the first and second floors. The house was sold in 1986.

With the growing needs for elder housing in Morristown, Father Dericks applied for and received town approval to convert the former convent at Macculloch Avenue and Perry Street into a residence for thirty seniors. It was dedicated in 1984. Today there is no longer a need for a parish convent, and the one remaining sister, Principal Merris Larkin, lives off-site.

The growing opportunities for women beyond traditional roles have adversely affected the number of religious vocations. However, as Sister June recalls, "The Sisters of Charity have cared for others whatever the need and type of job. Our roles continue to expand in today's world."

the
MINISTRY
CENTER

Dedicated to

*the many who devote hours of their lives
to Assumption's sick, poor, and bereaved, to religious education,
and to the lay support activities so crucial
to the smooth operation of our vibrant parish.*

Assumption's Ministry Center has served many purposes in its long lifetime and is now the hub of the many outreach programs and religious education activities.

Assumption Parish Files

The large white structure at 70 Macculloch Avenue has served many in its lifetime. Assumption purchased it from the Ballantine family in 1916 to serve as a convent for the Sisters of Charity who taught in our parish school. It later served as a novitiate for the order. In 1984 it was retrofitted to become much-needed housing for thirty Morristown community seniors; and it now is the center of the parish's ministries and outreach to hundreds of people each year.

From the early days of the parish through the Fifties, most of Assumption's lay organizations were dedicated to the spiritual and social needs of parishioners as exemplified by the activities of the Rosary Society, the Altar Society, CYO, Knights of Columbus, Holy Name Society, Mothers' Guild, and various Sodalities.

However, Vatican II invited the laity into the sanctuary—literally and figuratively—to adopt a more intimate relationship with the church and its sacred rites by serving as Eucharistic ministers, lectors, and the permanent diaconate. Lay congregants could now lead RCIA and Marriage Encounter groups, religious education programs, and outreach to the sick and the poor. Of course, the traditional service roles of ushering, music ministry, altar service, and altar linen care continued to thrive at Assumption.

One of the areas in which the impact of Vatican II was most felt was the reinstitution of the permanent diaconate after more than a millennium. All Catholic priests proceed through a period of the transitional diaconate on their way to ordination; however, the permanent diaconate was reintroduced for lay men who, after completing the course of study and preparation, are ordained deacons for the remainder of their lives.

On June 9, 1974, Gabriel Lasch was the first Assumption lay man to become a permanent deacon. A week later, he served as deacon for the first time at a Mass celebrated by his son, Monsignor Kenneth Lasch.

Deacon Lasch was followed by William (Bill) Harty and Anthony (Tony) DiLorenzo. Added to the growing roster of parish men called to this vocation were Frank Para, Mike Hanly, Tom Spruiell, Richard Pinto, James Butkus, and Brian Beyerl. All were key figures in the various rites and ministries they performed and led in the care of the Assumption flock.

Under the guidance of Sister Pat Marks and Sister Marie Graziano, Religious Education programs prospered. Religious Education includes instruction for children in grades one through eight who do not attend Assumption School, Confirmation preparation for freshmen and sophomores of the parish, the Catechesis of the Good Shepherd for children as young as three and one-half, and Service of the Word for Children. Presently, under the direction of Linda Macios, more than 700 children and youth of the parish are served by ninety volunteer catechists in our Religious Education Program whose motto is "Partnering with Parents." Religious Education now includes classes for special needs students as well as a program geared towards families called Fridays, Faith, and Family.

In 1996, the growth of the number of high school students in the parish warranted the employment of a part-time youth minister, Artie Flinn. He developed a peer minister program whereby juniors and seniors of the parish ministry became involved in the preparation of freshmen and sophomores for the Rite of Confirmation. In addition to their summer outreach to the impoverished families living in the Appalachia region of West Virginia, Youth Ministry—currently under the direction of Lisa Sullivan—participates in social and community service throughout the year. In 2005, the ever-vibrant Youth Ministry brought about the addition of the 5:30 p.m. Sunday Youth Mass, celebrated weekly September through May.

Sister of Charity Pat Godri worked at Assumption from 1991 to 1994 as a pastoral associate, ministering to hospitalized and homebound parishioners and supporting ministries to senior citizens, young adults, and RCIA candidates. As time elapsed, lay people took on expanded roles in these ministries. With the expansion of the principal ministries, more and more individuals became involved. As of 2011 Assumption has thirty-five ministry groups populated by hundreds of lay volunteers who serve not just our parish but the community at large, as indicated by the following roster.

Current Ministries at Assumption

Africa Surgery
Altar Linens
Altar Servers
Bereavement
Bethany
Boy Scouts
Cub Scouts
Centering Prayer
Children's Worship
Christian Service
CYO Basketball
Deaf Ministry
Eucharistic Ministry
Finance Committee
Food Pantry
Gardening
Good Samaritan
Holistic Health
Home and School
Interfaith Shelter
Just Faith
Knights of Columbus
Lectors
Moms and Tots
Nursing Homes
Pre-Cana
RCIA
Respect Life
Senior Citizens
Soup Kitchen
Ushers
Vocations
Why Catholic?
Young Adult
Youth Ministry

Between 2002 and 2005, a Golden Honor Roll was established "for dedicated service to our church community." Parishioners were named to the roster each year. The recipients of this honor are listed below in alphabetical order, not the chronological order in which they were named.

Bernice Anglin

Ray Dean

Sr. Gertrude Fitzsimmons

Sr. Marie Graziano

Deacon Bill and Claire Harty

John Ned Hines

Carole Hires

Julie Jennings

Joan Kramer

Deacon Gabe Lasch

Louise Madden

Fran Mandusky

Sister Pat Marks

Dorothea McDonough

Dave and Irene Phelan

Joycelyn Rigassio

Anthony Romano

JoAnne Smith

Frank Tozzi

The Dolores Hulvat Catechetical Award is presented each year in memory of Dolores Hulvat, who worked for more than twenty-five years as a catechist in the Archdiocese of Chicago and later here in Morristown and who was also involved in numerous projects in town. She died in 1997, but her memory lives through those who are honored for their dedication to the faith formation of the children and youth of the parish. Recipients are

1997	Msgr. Martin F. Rauscher
1998	Barbara Knehr
1999	Frank and Pat Para
2000	Judy Perry
2001	Sister Marie Graziano
2002	John and Joan Barbarula
2003	Sister Gertrude Fitzsimmons
2004	Nancy Delaney
2005	The "Founding Mothers" of Catechesis of the Good Shepherd: Sister Pat Marks, Sister Marie Graziano, JuliAnn Ferdenzi, Marianna Quagliano, Mary Romance
2006	Liz Wilkey
2007	Michele Para
2008	Pam Johnson
2009	Claudia Nardi
2010	Deacon Mike Hanly

A reading of the current list of thirty-five ministries demonstrates the degree to which Assumption parishioners are devoting time and energy to performing both the corporal and spiritual works of mercy. It also underscores the variety of talents and interests of the hundreds of volunteers who propel the work of these wide-ranging ministries. As stated earlier, these organizations have evolved from having a strictly kinship and/or spiritual focus to contributing to the added outreach and support of many in our parish and community. Social ministries and religious education have joined traditional liturgical services support to make our Ministry Center, along with its satellite sites, the vibrant gathering place it is today.

the CEMETERY

Dedicated to

*the many who rest in the consecrated ground of
Holy Rood and to the former parishioners buried
throughout the world.*

Entrance to the main gate of Holy
Rood Cemetery.

Assumption Parish Files

One of the corporal works of mercy is burying the dead, and from its inception the Church of the Assumption has accomplished this by establishing a Catholic cemetery, originally within the churchyard and later in the Morristown environs.

What is today the upper parking lot of the church was the site of the original graveyard, purchased in 1861 from William Collins for $500. As the small cemetery reached its capacity, sixteen acres fronting Whippany and Columbia Roads were purchased in 1875 to become the new cemetery, Holy Rood (meaning Holy Cross).

In 1886 excavation began on the property in use by the old cemetery for the first free-standing parish school. The interred bodies were moved to Holy Rood by friends of the deceased, if any remained, or under the personal supervision of the pastor. The same year, a vault was constructed at Holy Rood to hold bodies awaiting burial in cases of emergencies and epidemics. This became an important addition in light of the pneumonia and influenza epidemics and pandemics that plagued the country in later years.

Throughout the 1960s and 1970s, Holy Rood underwent enhancement and enlargement. Perpetual care had been introduced in 1968 and, when a new section of the cemetery was opened that same year, all plots began to be sold with that

Resplendent in the chapel of the third mausoleum are three stained glass windows, depicting the nativity, resurrection, and ascension of Christ, that date back to 1882.

© Sergio Burani—Photos by Sergio

service. A cinderblock house, purchased from the State of New Jersey, was moved to Holy Rood in 1972 to serve as the caretaker's house.

A mausoleum containing 478 crypt burial spaces was begun in 1976, and it was dedicated on May 29, 1977. Erection of a second mausoleum was initiated in 1983 and a third (the highest of the trio on the upper hill) in the mid-Nineties. Three stained glass windows that once graced All Souls Hospital, originally located on Mount Kemble Avenue and built by Assumption pastor Father Joseph Flynn in 1882, were installed in the third mausoleum in 1996. Morristown Memorial Hospital donated these windows, designed by Mayer Brothers of Munich and London (creators of the stained glass windows in our church) to Assumption.

The fourth mausoleum, located on the lower level near the office, was completed in 2005, bringing the total number of crypts to 1,721 (for above-ground burials) and 272 niches (for cremains). All of the mausoleums provide meditation areas and chapels for those wishing to pray for and remember their deceased.

As of 2011 over 12,000 people are interred in Holy Rood. While burial in our cemetery is available to all area Catholics, the majority of those who rest there were once Assumption parishioners. Also interred are former pastors, including Father James Sheeran (reputed to be the only Confederate chaplain buried in a Northern cemetery), and several members of Paul Revere's family.

Holy Rood has changed dramatically from the pastoral meadows that were purchased in 1875 to accommodate the remains of early Assumptionites. However, the same peace and aura of eternal rest permeate these consecrated grounds today.

the
ART

Dedicated to

all things beautiful.

the ART

Guide to the statuary and sculptures

A great deal of the beauty that graces the Church of the Assumption is lent by iconic art. The sculptured pieces, stained glass windows, Stations of the Cross, and sacred vessels are not in place just for the sake of adornment but are integral to our rituals, represent some tenet of our faith, or honor saints who demonstrated heroic practice of Catholicism during their lives.

The following photographs from Assumption's parish files and other cited sources highlight only the major art pieces found within the church that add to the beauty and devotion of our many services.

© Sergio Burani—Photos by Sergio

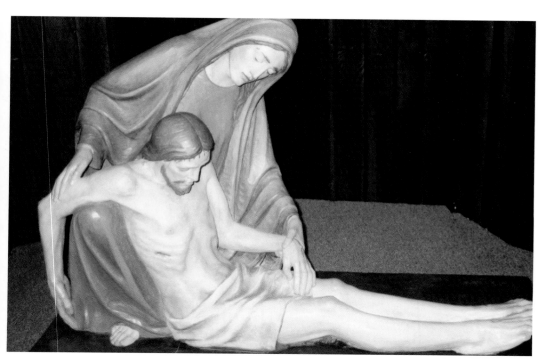

(upper)
Carved in Italy and installed in Assumption on April 1, 1974, this **Pieta** replaced the original plaster 1887 version. This second Pieta was modeled from a picture of a small marble replica in Bishop Casey's residence. It resides at the left side entrance but is moved into the main church during Lent.

(lower)
Statues of **St. Patrick, St. Ann and the Child Mary**, and **St. Anthony** are located in the alcove opposite the Pieta at the side entrance.

opposite page:
(far left)
The **Statue of the Sacred Heart of Jesus** dates back to 1875. It is located in the niche on the left side of the main church.

(upper right)
The **Statue of the Assumption of the Blessed Virgin Mary** was imported from Italy in 1907. It is currently backed by the fleurs-de-lis mural located on the front right side of the church.

(lower right)
The **Statue of Saint Joseph** dates back to the 1948 renovation of the church. It currently rests in a niche on the right side of the church.

The Statue of St. Therese of Lisieux, restored by the Long family in memory of their daughter Hannah, is found in the entryway to the parish community room. Records indicate the statue first arrived at Assumption in 1972.

© Sergio Burani—Photos by Sergio

The Holy Family statue was purchased when the parish community room was built. It is located at the entrance across from the St. Therese statue.

© Sergio Burani—Photos by Sergio

The Blessed Mother with Children of the World, a work in high relief on a background panel, was purchased for a wall in the parish community room.

Details of the new crucifix, installed on
April 15, 2011.

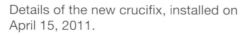

The Baptistry, introduced with the 2007 renovation of the church.

This Easter 2011 photo displays the current tabernacle, adoring angels, the sanctuary lamp, and what is believed to be the original crucifix.

© Sergio Burani—Photos by Sergio

Our Stations of the Cross were created in 1892 by Carbane of Paris. They were painted on copper and later enameled. When they needed repair in 1969, the artist reversed the copper, painting the side that was imprinted. The former front (now the back) can be viewed if the entire station is reversed.

the WINDOWS

Guide to the stained glass windows

The following descriptions of the original stained glass windows that grace the Church of the Assumption are excerpts from Father Flynn's book *The Story of a Parish*, pp. 278-281. They detail "the generosity of those who have contributed so much to the beautifying of our Church." All but those in the choir loft, the sacristy, the reconciliation room, the connector hall, and right alcove were created by Mayer and Company of Munich. They were installed in stages between 1882 and 1906 and bear the imprint "Mayer & Company, London & Munich."

Most of these original windows described below appeared in the *1976 Assumption Bicentennial History of Catholic America* (Custom Book). The photographer for the newer windows is identified under the appropriate images.

In St. Joseph's aisle, the west side of the Church and over the confessional are St. John and St. Vincent de Paul, with the emblem of a dove bearing an olive-branch in its beak. It is the gift of Patrick Welsh and wife, in memory of their son: "To the memory of John V. Welsh, died January 11, 1883, aged ten years."

Shipped from Munich March 14, 1885

With the passion-flower above is the window of St. Virgil, Bishop and Abbot of Saltzburg, and St. Brigid of Ireland, bearing in hand the lighted lamp. This was erected by the Young Ladies' Sodality to the memory of Sister Gaudentia [first Sister of Charity principal, aka Sister-Servant]: *"Eternal rest grant, O Lord, to Sister Gaudentia. June 11, 1884."*

The other to Father Henry [a young diocesan priest who spent his last month of life at our rectory in attempt to regain his health]: *"Eternal rest, O Lord, grant to Rev. Arthur J. Henry. September 6, 1880."*

Shipped from Munich on March 14, 1885

The Purgatory window is the gift of Bessie Carroll and Bridget Quinn. The Sacred Heart of Jesus is emblazoned above the figures of St. Michael and Our Lady, Comfortress of the Afflicted. The inscription reads

"May the souls of the faithful departed, through the mercy of God, rest in peace. Amen."

Shipped from Munich on November 18, 1886

The School Children, in 1887, raised the money to put in the window which represents Jesus blessing the little ones whom the mother brings to Him. The Gospel text recalls it: *"Suffer little children to come unto me. By the School Children, 1887."* The symbol is a seraph.

Shipped from Munich on May 20, 1887

The Rosary Society contributed the money for the beautiful window which represents Our Lady and the Divine Infant presenting the Rosary to St. Dominic.

The symbol is the dog, bearing the torch and a globe. The motive which inspired the Rosarians is embodied in the following: *"To the Queen of the Most Holy Rosary. A loving tribute from the Rosary Society, 1887. Pray for us."*

Shipped from Munich on May 20, 1887

Mrs. Ellen Eakely and her daughters perpetuate the memory of their relatives in the window which contains figures of St. Thomas the Apostle and St. Helena with a cluster of grapes and wheat as emblems.

"In loving memory of Thomas Degan, died November 4, 1887. Ellen Degen, died January 16, 1887. May they rest in peace."

Shipped from Munich on July 21, 1888

James Lonergan, in affectionate remembrance of his parents, donated the window in which St. Leo the Great and St. Rose of Lima are represented. The emblem is the lamb and Book of Seven Seals. The inscription is

"Jesu, have mercy on James Lonegan, died January 1, 1887. Bridget Lonegan, died July 10, 1873."

Shipped from Munich on July 21, 1888

The window containing the figures of St. Paul of the Cross and St. Francis deSales with the emblem of a chalice and host read

"Merciful Jesu, spare thy servant, William Nelson Wood, who died full of peace and hope, April 17, 1880."

Shipped from Munich on July 21, 1888

The window of St. Joseph and St. Patrick was placed by Patrick Farrelly and wife to the memory of their son. At the base is

"In loving memory of Joseph Patrick Farrelly, died April 21, 1887. In thy mercy, Jesu, spare him and all Christian souls." The emblem is the Sun of Justice.

Shipped from Munich on July 26, 1887

The window of St. Ann and the infant Virgin and St. Bernard, with the crown as an emblem, is the gift of Mrs. M. Howard, and is inscribed

"In memory of Ann Martin, died March 4, 1878. Loving Jesu, grant her eternal rest."

Shipped from Munich on May 20, 1887

Next is the window of St. Monica and St. Augustine, the gift of Mrs. L. Robeson. A bunch of lilies is in the little rose window and the inscription reads

"Daniel Augustine Robeson, died September 20, 1869. Sweet Jesu, grant him and us everlasting life."

Shipped from Munich on November 18, 1886

On the [left] of Father Sheeran's window is that of St. Henry and St. Agnes, with the emblem, an anchor. This is the gift of Mrs. Agnes Kelly, and it bears the inscription

"To the glory of God, and in loving memory of the deceased husband of Agnes Kelly, A.D. 1886."

Shipped from Munich on February 15, 1886

The Father Sheeran Memorial [depicts St. Alphonsus Liguori and St. James the Apostle and] bears above the symbol of the pelican, and beneath the inscription

"To the memory of Rev. James Sheeran, who crowned a life of zeal, energy, and labor by the erection of this Church. Rich in good works, he slept in the Lord April 3, 1881. Jesu, grant him eternal rest. Amen."

Shipped from Munich on September 13, 1882

To the [right] are the beautiful cherubs to the memory of
"John Carr, died November 27, 1876. James Carr, died
June 16, 1878." These are the gift of John A. Carr.

Shipped from Munich on March 14, 1885

Father Flynn did not specifically describe the Mayer & Company stained glass windows located elsewhere in the church, but this record would be incomplete without detailing what is known of them.

These three windows are installed above the church entrance into the Parish Center.
Shipped from Munich on September 13, 1882

St. Catherine, Martyr *(left)*
"To the memory of Daisy Farrelly, died December 10, 1876."

Guardian Angel *(center)*
"To the memory of our little angel, died October 1, 1877."

St. Elizabeth *(right)*
"To the memory of Maude Farrelly, died July 23, 1876."

The sanctuary windows have been a focal point of devotion and beauty since the turn of the Twentieth Century. They were restored later during one of the church's renovations.

© Sergio Burani—Photos by Sergio

The Annunciation (left)
"Donated by L.J. O'Connor; restored by W. Nelson Wood."
Shipped from Munich on October 27, 1906

The Marriage of Mary And Joseph (second)
"Donated by Margaret Lowenstein; restored by W. Nelson Wood."
Shipped from Munich on October 27, 1906

The Assumption of The Blessed Virgin Mary (center) "Restored"
This centerpiece window depicting our patroness was the first stained glass window installed over the altar.
Shipped from Munich on July 26, 1887

The Nativity (fourth)
"Donated by Margery Durning; restored by Margaret Healy."
Shipped from Munich on October 27, 1906

The Wedding Feast of Cana (right)
"Donated by Mary Russell; restored by Hannah Anglin."
Shipped from Munich on October 27, 1906

Two smaller Mayer & Company stained glass windows can be found in the back corners of the church. *Both shipped from Munich on July 21, 1888*

St. Margaret of Scotland
(located in the Ushers' Room)
"In thy mercy, Jesu, grant rest and peace to Margaret Whelan."

St. Cecilia
(located at the bottom of the choir loft stairs)
"May God have mercy on Margaret Whelan, died May 6, 1888."

© Sergio Burani—Photos by Sergio

Not all of our stained glass windows date back to the early days of our parish. The newer pieces, identified below, were created by Hiemer & Company of Clifton, New Jersey.

Installed in 1956 by Hiemer & Company, this series of four windows was painted by Basque artist Simon Berasaluce, whose name graces a Spanish square in his hometown. They were destroyed by the 1985 fire but could be reconstructed from the original plans still held by Hiemer & Company.

Choir Loft (the Rose Window)
The centerpiece of this beautiful work depicts Our Lady of Fatima surrounded by symbols of Christ and the Holy Eucharist.

(under the Rose Window)
King David *(left)* *"A gift of the Holy Name Society."*
St. Pius X *(center)* *"In memory of deceased relatives of the Sullivan family"*
St. Cecilia *(right)* *"A gift of the Rosary Society."*

St. Joseph and the Child Jesus
Another Mayer & Company stained glass window was ordered by Father Flynn for his study in the then-new (our current) rectory. This work arrived shortly after the priests moved into the rectory in 1890 and remains in place in the first-floor study.

Shipped from Munich on December 3, 1890

These windows were created and installed by Hiemer & Company in 1958.

Our Lady of Fatima, located in the sacristy.

The Eucharist, located to the right of the statue of the Assumption of the Blessed Virgin Mary.

This Hiemer & Company window, entitled **The Keys to the Kingdom**, was installed in 1958 along with those depicting The Eucharist and Our Lady of Fatima on the previous page. Located in the sacristy, it was probably covered over when the Parish Center was added to the church, as it is no longer visible.

The Baptism of Christ (left) located in the Reconciliation Room.
"In memory of Lillian Andreorio."

These Marian windows, installed in 2005 by Hiemer & Company, were underwritten by an anonymous donor as part of the Parish Center construction.

The windows are located in the connector hallway between the church and the community room.

Queen of Peace *(left)*
Queen of the Rosary *(center)*
Cause of Our Joy *(right)*

the
REMINISCENCES

Dedicated to

the memories we share and those we
hold close to our hearts.

A number of clergy, religious, and long-time parishioners accepted the invitation to share a memory or two of life at Assumption.

We hope these remembrances will provide interesting reading and, perhaps, trigger readers' own memories of life in this special parish.

"Assumption Parish has filled my life with fond memories. When people truly love one another the way Assumption people do, you have a peaceful environment in which to live. Whenever I asked the people for help or service, they always came through. They always went the extra twenty miles in their effort. Assumption is Worshiping God, Serving the Needy and the Poor, and Sharing Fellowship in a Loving Community. That is as good as it gets. I promise all the parishioners my prayers, and I ask them to keep me in their prayers.

"I look forward to a great homecoming and celebration with God and all His people who love Him."

Msgr. Martin Rauscher, Native Son, Pastor Emeritus
Assumption Pastor, 1990-2009

"I was a very young child when we joined Assumption in 1936. My parents sat on the Blessed Virgin's side in the third row. A pulpit hung on the front column and the pastor [Father Barrett] gave his homilies above us. I believe the Stations of the Cross currently in the church are the ones we used when I was a child—they are very old. I graduated from the parish schools, took all my childhood sacraments there, and was ordained at the Cathedral in Paterson.

"In my memory, I can still see the school with classrooms and the gym surrounding a courtyard, and I can remember the old liturgy we followed during Mass. I was an altar server in the old days when the priest would read the epistle on the right side of the altar, signal the server, and we had to carry the Book to the left side of the altar where he would read the gospel of the day—in Latin, of course."

Father Joseph Casey, Native Son
Parishioner from 1936-2011
Retired Priest of the Paterson Diocese
Died July 25, 2011

"As an altar server [at Assumption], I remember the quiet of the sacristy when I arrived on my bike to prepare for the 6:30 a.m. Mass. With bated breath, I would wait for the priest 'on duty,' hoping that it would not be the pastor—who was not as patient with us neophyte servers.

"I also recall creating quite a stir after serving Mass. I was putting the altar cards and other altar items in the storage area behind the main altar when all of a sudden I accidentally kicked one of the flower stands behind the very heavy double-tiered branch candles. The plants cascaded into a large bronze vase of flowers and then into the branch candles, which then crashed to the marble floor. The very patient Father Jim Daly simply quietly reviewed the situation and instructed me to clean it up. Not another word was spoken. The lower tier of the branch candles is just a bit crooked to this day!

"In the olden days, Catholic schools had no school buses, and so we walked the distance to school, many of us over a mile, but we were none the worse for wear.

"The parish was the spiritual and social center of our lives as Catholics. There were movies and shows and, of course, CYO sports in the small gym on Madison Street.

"And the priests used to take up the collection at Sunday Mass!"

Msgr. Kenneth E. Lasch, Native Son
Retired Priest of the Paterson Diocese

"It is always a blessing to find oneself assigned to a parochial ministry that is both rewarding and fulfilling, as have been my years at Assumption. Under the leadership of both Father Martin Rauscher and Father John Hart, Assumption is a parish that is particularly vibrant and challenging. The many ministries, from the liturgical to the social service, are constantly evolving. My days are full and rich with new and ever-changing dynamics in the realm of spirituality, service and blessing. All aspects of ministry at Assumption are dynamic and call for an ever-changing response in terms of leadership and growth. From cradle to grave the full spectrum of the spiritual life is dramatically present and calls for a response that stretches all community members to the maximum. I will forever be grateful for the wonderful opportunities that my service here at Assumption has provided me."

Father Dennis Crowley
Associate Pastor from 1991 to 2011

"My personal recollections of Assumption Parish, Morristown, go back to pastor Father Francis Doogan (1954-1966), who had been pastor of St. Cecilia's, Rockaway (1940-1946), in my high school years. I served Mass for him, and in 1943 he recommended me for acceptance as a candidate for the priesthood by Bishop McLaughlin, our first Bishop of Paterson (1938-1947). Father Doogan was still at St. Cecilia's when I went off to the minor seminary, St. Charles College, Catonsville, MD, in 1944. One of the most pleasant things I remember the priests at Assumption saying about him was that he responded with a donation to every missionary or religious request made of him.

"As Bishop of Paterson I appointed as Assumption's pastor Rev. Michael J. Conway to succeed Rev. John H. Dericks in 1986; and to succeed Rev. Conway I appointed Rev. Martin Rauscher in 1990 (all three pastors were later named monsignors by Pope John Paul II). I also appointed Father Mark J. Olenowski, parochial vicar of Assumption, as his first assignment in 1985, and Father Dennis Crowley for that same pastoral service in 1991. The present pastor, Msgr. John E. Hart, I ordained to the priesthood and later assigned him as my priest secretary and diocesan chancellor.

"Through my twenty-six years as Bishop of Paterson I celebrated Confirmation liturgies each year in the parish and the rededication Masses after the tragic fire and the beautiful renovations under Monsignor Rauscher, as well as the dedication of the converted historic convent on Macculloch Avenue into the Dericks Residence. Through all the years one of the outstanding memories I have of Assumption Parish is the emphasis the priests, deacons, religious, lay ministers, and the congregation put on the liturgy, especially music, and on youth ministry, including the outstanding school, religious education program, and the preparation of the candidates for confirmation.

"Assumption Parish may be old in years but it is still young in spirit, a vibrant family of Jesus' faithful disciples."

Most Rev. Frank J. Rodimer
Ordained Sixth Bishop of Paterson on February 28, 1978
Retired June 1, 2004

"It was Wednesday, April 10th, and we had just celebrated Easter Sunday three days earlier. I was having a cup of tea in the rectory kitchen with Marc McGinnis, minister of music. The doorbell rang, and I answered it. A man stood there and blurted out, 'The church is on fire!' I saw the smoke from the doorway, and my heart leaped with the danger. I ran to the phone and called 911 to report the fire.

"Marc and I ran to the church. I looked up at the roof and could see flames over the choir loft. Marc and I began to take things out of the church and remove them to the safety of the rectory. I emptied the tabernacle of the consecrated hosts and removed the Blessed Sacrament to the rectory. We began to remove kneelers, vestments, chalices, sacramentaries, hymnals, and other liturgical objects. We removed the chairs on the altar and anything else that was not bolted down.

"Within five minutes the police showed up and a few minutes later the fire engines arrived. The firemen spread out and began to determine how to get water on *the dancing flames as they began to crackle. The church was over one hundred years old and the dry wood of the roof would burn quickly. The firemen had to punch a hole in the beautiful stained glass rose window. As I watched from below I saw the flames begin to creep down the nave from the choir loft towards the sanctuary. Soon flaming embers began to fall from the roof onto the pews. It was enough to reduce me to tears.*

"Within fifteen minutes parishioners and local people began to assemble and offer assistance. They helped to remove whatever else was left in the church before the fire reduced it to ashes. Monsignor John Dericks, the pastor, had left for his day off earlier in the evening, and it took some time to reach him. When he arrived at 11:30 p.m. the flames were shooting skywards, and the whole area around the church was a fiery red glow.

"The fire burned for some hours, and the entire roof was lost before the fire was brought under control. By 1:30 a.m. the fire had burned out, and we were able to get some sleep. The sacristy area and daily Mass chapel were not severely affected, but the smell of smoke was very strong. The next day we met with diocesan officials to determine the cost of the fire and how the church would be rebuilt.

"Fire officials began to examine the cause of the fire. It was quickly determined where the fire began, over the choir loft. At the time, the church was to be air-conditioned and the contractor had taken a high-wattage bulb out of its protective casing in the ceiling. The bulb was then draped over a rafter and left there. When the organist had practiced earlier that evening, the lights were turned on; as the bulb over the rafter shone its light, the rafter began to smolder from the heat of the bulb. Less than one hour later the rafter caught fire and the church fire broke out.

"The clean-up and restoration turned out to be a lengthy process. Each weekend the gym in the school was used for the liturgies. The church was rebuilt and eventually was refurbished to reflect great beauty.

"I was privileged to serve at Assumption Parish for some ten years as associate pastor, from 1975 to 1985. I left to become campus minister at the College of St. Elizabeth. I was able to be present when the church was reopened in 1986 for liturgy. I pray that Assumption Church will continue to provide spiritual guidance and a welcoming space in Morristown for generations to come."

Rev. Christopher Muldoon
Pastor, Our Lady Star of the Sea, Lake Hopatcong, NJ
Associate Pastor, Assumption, 1975—1985

"God has been wonderfully good to us in countless ways. Near the top of the list has been our experience as active members of Assumption. Assumption School has always excelled in its mission to educate our children and grandchildren. Our many priests and sisters have always inspired, enlightened, and consoled us.

"There is an ad for a chain of restaurants that says, 'When you're here, you're family.' That is so true of Assumption Parish. Through the years we have had many people say to us that when they first entered our church they felt so very much at home. That is how it has been for us through the years."

Deacon Bill and Claire Harty
Parishioners since 1953
Bill, a Deacon since 1986

"I have been a parishioner at Assumption for almost thirty years, and I've loved every minute of it. I think the clergy, the staff, and the people of Assumption are the best. In 1981, Father Conway supported my entering diaconate formation. In 1989 Father Martin reconfirmed that support. Through nineteen years as a deacon, it has been my privilege and joy to officiate at 500+ baptisms and forty-plus weddings. I'm also honored to allow God to share his thoughts through me in the many homilies I've given. I'm also gratified to be with our parishioners in times of grief during wake, funeral, and graveside services. Jeanne and I are very happy to have coordinated the Pre-Cana Ministry for eighteen years. It was a privilege to meet with and converse with all those young couples about the beauty and sanctity of the Sacrament of Matrimony. It was also an honor to coordinate the Respect Life Ministry for ten years.

"One of my true joys was my involvement in the CCD program. For eight years, Jeanne and I were catechists in the classroom. For the last ten years, I have been the 'Roving Deacon.' The Director of Religious Education (Linda Macios) would develop a schedule where, on Sunday mornings and sometimes Sunday evenings, I would put on my vestments and teach one of the class lessons, lead a prayer service in the little theatre, or conduct a tour of the church. It was and is an honor to bring the teachings of Christ to these young minds.

"I have been blessed with very supportive clergy, from Father Dericks and Father Mike Conway to Father Martin, Father Dennis, and Father John Hart. Everyone at Assumption has always been very gracious to and supportive of me. I will always treasure my time at Assumption."

Deacon Mike Hanly
Parishioner since 1984
Deacon since 1991

"My wife Andrea and I joined Assumption parish in 1987. We looked at most of the Catholic elementary schools in this area and were so impressed with Assumption School that we enrolled our children on the spot and chose Morristown as our home. I have been a deacon at Assumption since May 2007.

"The strengths of Assumption are its school, priests, and parishioners. I was raised in the Protestant church and converted to Catholicism when I married my wife Andrea—my first communion was on our wedding day. I thought I would blend into the 'spiritual woodwork' of the church, until Father Martin asked me to consider becoming a deacon about ten years ago. To this day I wonder why, but I guess the Lord works in mysterious ways.

"One thing is for sure, the Lord worked through Father Martin as our pastor. Father Martin has a wonderfully simple and straightforward faith. He told me once, 'You know, Brian, this faith stuff isn't hard at all. I ask the Lord to help me every day, and, if he does, I thank Him and ask Him for the same thing the next day!' I loved to ask Father Martin to define certain spiritual concepts, because I knew he could 'cut to the chase' and simplify the concept. I asked him once to define 'sacrament.' His answer: 'An encounter with God.' I never underestimated the spiritual significance of Eucharist or confession after that! We at Assumption are continually blessed by our priests. Fathers Ken Lasch, Dennis Crowley, and John Hart are the best of the best—it is a great privilege to have them at Assumption.

"The other strength of Assumption is the faith and compassion of its parishioners. Recently my mother passed away in Florida. I have been overwhelmed by the prayers and support that I've received from my fellow parishioners. The Mass

cards keep coming. Assumption parishioners have strong faith and even stronger love. It has been a tremendous blessing to be a deacon at Assumption. The parishioners continue to inspire me with their faith and support.

"May God continue to richly bless Assumption Parish!"

Deacon Brian Beyerl
Parishioner since 1987
Deacon since 2007

"I joined Assumption School's teaching staff in September 1979, taught for fifteen years, and in 1995 became principal.

"Assumption was a wonderful school when I arrived, and we're blessed to be able to say the same thing thirty-one years later. I have been lucky enough to work with very special and supportive pastors—Father Martin and Father John. Having pastors who appreciate the importance of having a parish school is key to our success."

Sister Merris Larkin, SC
Teaching sister at Assumption from 1979 to 1995
Assumption Principal since 1995

"During my many years at Assumption, the parishioners had great faith, big hearts, and a wonderful spirit of dedication. Nothing was too difficult. As they saw one thing accomplished, they would dedicate themselves to the next, no matter how strenuous or unattainable it seemed. They always succeeded. I remember that many of the fund-raising projects, such as the fashion show, had humble beginnings. The first year there were only forty-nine attendees, but the participants and donors had a marvelous time...and look how that event has grown!

"As an educator, I have held a firm belief that student self-confidence is essential to his or her success in any undertaking, including academics. That is why I introduced them to an inspiration attributable to Walt Whitman: 'I am larger, better than I thought; I did not know I held so much goodness.' That is an important

insight for us to instill in our students, and I believe those words still appear in the entrance hall of Assumption School. Our young people need to hear and see such reinforcement frequently."

June Morrissey, SC
Assumption Principal, 1973-1995

"On January 27, 1947, I was assigned to teach the first grade at Bayley School in Morristown. It was my first mission, and I was to join the sisters who were teaching in the school. The convent was known as Saint Mary Convent, situated at the corner of Perry Street and Macculloch Avenue. Eight of the sisters taught the grammar grades; five sisters taught in the high school. There were several lay teachers also teaching. There was a nurse, who was a dedicated and much-loved person.

"The grammar school building was the only one of its kind in this part of the county. It was built in the late 1800s, architecture being reminiscent of the old English country school. There was an open school yard where the church parking lot exists now. That's where the students lined up, according to grade, and filed through the gated entry, which led to a square, cement courtyard. Framing the courtyard was a wooden platform, reminiscent of the western movies where the cowboys hitched their horses to a hitching post and entered a particular building. Each classroom had its own entry from the platform. The lower grades occupied the first floor; most higher grades were located on the second floor.

"There was no hallway, and the lavatories were entered from the platform. There were no radiators in the lavatories—they were mighty cold in the winter! However, there was an indescribable charm about this unusual school. Everyone knew everyone. The neighborhood was nicknamed "Dublin," and in some ways we experienced life in the 1800s.

"In 1949 there was a new faculty and a new principal, Sister Catherine Gertrude, who introduced innovations that were preparatory to an increased number of children entering Bayley School. She introduced uniforms for both boys and girls. This created a more formal atmosphere in the classrooms. A church choir brought to light the talents that existed in the school. She started a kindergarten class, which increased the enrollment, and created a Mothers' Guild—a wonderful group that enhanced the social dynamics. There was no end to the energy generated by these wonderful mothers, and they did so much for the Bayley School.

"The Fifties ushered in a new era in our society. New businesses emerged. Fathers were transferred out of and into our districts. The population was becoming transient, and the Baby Boomers were entering kindergarten, thus causing needs for new accommodations.

"Monsignor Edward Barrett was the pastor during these years. He was cognizant of the changes in our society, and he had been preparing for the influx of students and the necessity of erecting a new school. Being a member of the Building and Sites Committee for the Paterson Diocese, he had a keen sense of the value of land. He purchased a beautiful piece of property on Macculloch Avenue across the street from the convent. It had been the Parker estate, owned by a Judge Parker. It was at this location that the new school was erected and named Assumption School. Because of the added numbers of pupils in 1959, the new school had two sections of each grade, and lay teachers were hired to conduct the extra classes.

"Monsignor Barrett did not live to see the fruition of his plans and this great contribution to the Assumption Parish. He passed away in December 1953 and is buried in front of Assumption Church.

"Father Francis Doogan followed Monsignor Barrett, and the construction began soon after. He oversaw the praiseworthy edifice that is now Assumption School. It continues to thrive as a school of choice and has a wonderful reputation."

Kathleen Murphy, SC (Sister Mary Roseaire)
Teaching Sister at Assumption from 1947—1964

"In 1978 I was studying at Drew Graduate School in the PhD program, Religion and Psychology. At the time I also worked in Rose Memorial Library on that campus. I had heard that Monsignor Dericks was looking for a part-time coordinator of Religious Education. The program enrolled about 100 children. I accepted the job, and Sister Marie Graziano began teaching religion in Assumption School where Sister

June Morrissey was principal. I worked as coordinator from 1978 to 1982, took other jobs after that, and returned to Assumption in 1990, where I worked with religious education and the Good Shepherd Program until 2007. During that time the number of children in the religious education program grew to about 500. Sister Marie and I started the Children's Word service. As we grew older, we asked Linda Macios if she would sign on as staff member in training, which she did. Several others joined in this ministry.

"We consider ourselves very fortunate to have met and worked with such capable people as Linda Macios, Sharon Bertram, and Tara Speer. Their leadership has helped Assumption Religious Education to be the outstanding program it is today, and Father Martin was unfailingly supportive and was always willing to listen."

Sister Pat Marks
Assumption Ministry, 1978—2007

"My great-grandfather, Cornelius Holly [Hally], immigrated to Morristown from Ireland before Assumption Church was founded, sometime in the early 1840s. He fought in our Civil War. He married Bridgit Buggy, and family history tells of their settling in the Dublin area of Morristown, purchasing property along Madison Street, James Street and Macculloch Avenue. They were able to house many people during those many years, many of whom were Irish immigrants. One of those houses was 'The Beehive,' aka 'The Big House.' I am told that, before the church was built, a priest would travel to Morristown on occasion and celebrate Mass in one of the homes for all the many Catholics in the neighborhood. Eventually my family sold all of that property.

"My grandparents and parents also raised their families here and Assumption was, of course, our parish. My parents both attended the old Bayley Grammar and High Schools; I attended Bayley Grammar and Bayley-Ellard High. During the 1920s Assumption had a very good adult choir. My grandmother, Mary Holly Keating, and my cousin, Jane Holly, sang with the choir. As a reward for the choir's hard work, the pastor treated all the members to a day at the Belmar shore each summer.

"One of my happiest days was when I made my confirmation in 1953. Archbishop Boland officiated. To prepare for the big day, we had to memorize answers

to 100 printed questions about the Church and our beliefs. How I crammed. Early each morning, my mother tested me. At school, Sister quizzed my confirmation class first thing after morning prayer. In the evening my friend from next door helped me. After all, the Archbishop might ask me a question that I would not know, much to the disgrace of my family and school! All of that preparation plus the excitement of buying a new dress and choosing a confirmation name made that day an unforgettable experience.

"When he died, Father Barrett was waked in the Assumption rectory for several days. Each school class was scheduled to spend a half-hour at the wake, so there was always a group of young students in the room with the body during the school day.

"May was always a very exciting month because of the Marian devotions. The pupils in each classroom built a shrine. The bases were fresh fruit and vegetable baskets gathered from local stores, and the trim was blue and white crepe paper. We children would supply fresh flowers and vases from our gardens throughout the month. If it was your turn to bring flowers, there was always a rush that morning to harvest them, make a bouquet and still be on time for the 8:00 mass. The finale of course was the May procession. We girls were dressed in white with blue trim dresses and wore fresh flowers in our hair. (Later we wore little hats.) Singing hymns, we would process from the Bayley School courtyard, up Madison Street onto Maple Avenue and into the church, where it was standing room only with many onlookers waiting outside. The girl who had been chosen to crown the Virgin Mary wore a bridal gown.

"Many of the sisters were very, very strict, but we students took it all in stride. There were few crybabies in those days. I believe that today Sister Merris leads Assumption School brilliantly. She is bright, articulate, and successfully navigates both the religious and secular worlds.

"One great thing about today's church is the access the laity has to the priests and religious. They are far more approachable and seem more aware of the reality and issues of living and working in the secular world. They no longer project the image of being far superior to the congregation; for example, the ability we have to call them by their first names. When we were young, we children didn't even know a priest's first name, much less be able to use it when we spoke to him!

"I was very upset when the Vatican II changes brought down the magnificent main altar and communion rail. The absence of that beautiful altar left a cavernous space in the sanctuary that could only be filled at Christmas with a lot of fir trees. However, the recent renovation of the church has totally changed the appearance of the sanctuary so it no longer looks empty and bare. The church is once again beautiful and inviting.

"The community room was absolutely needed and is the best thing we could do to build a sense of neighborhood in our parish, which has developed from a predominantly Irish population to a multicultural melting pot, as has the town. I think the Church is today softer and more responsive to the community at large. I am so proud to be a member of Assumption with a long family history in this parish.

Mary Louise Hallinan Smith, Native Daughter
Great-Granddaughter of a Founding Member and Life-Long Parishioner

"I was born in 1918 in Morristown; my family lived on Budd Street. My mother died when I was about seven years old, and my father was unable to keep the family together at that time. As a result, most of the children in our family were temporarily boarded out with neighboring families, and I went to St. Anthony's Home, an orphanage in Passaic. Monsignor Ellard was the pastor at Assumption during this period, and his kindness to us and other members of Assumption was extraordinary. He checked up on the children of my family to make sure we were well treated during our separation. I still remember Monsignor Ellard riding his horse, making a striking figure in his red riding outfit.

"Within a year or two my family was reunited, and we moved to Mount Kemble Avenue. I eventually married at Assumption and raised my own family here. You can say I am a life-long parishioner of Assumption."

Pauline DeChiaro
Life-Long Parishioner

"My parents moved into Assumption Parish when I was nine years old. We lived on Franklin Street before Morristown Memorial Hospital was located in that vicinity.

"Father Ellard was the pastor at that time, and he was a very kind man. He used to visit the people in Little Dublin. It was the time of the Great Depression, and he helped many in that neighborhood put food on their table—we suspected that he used his own money to do so. I have been a member of Assumption through seven pastorates: Ellard, Barrett, Doogan, Dericks, Conway, Rauscher, and Hart.

"Assumption has always been a special parish. I believe Catholics have melded well into community life, and society itself has become more tolerant of other cultures and religions. I can remember when in my youth one of my non-Catholic acquaintances asked me what church I attended. When I replied 'Assumption,' she exclaimed incredulously, 'You're a Catholic? You sure don't look like one.'"

Helen Hoyt
Parishioner since 1931

"My family became members of Assumption Parish when we moved to Morristown in the 1930s. One of my most treasured memories is when I was a Senior at Morristown High School in 1944 where I was a member of the highly acclaimed A Cappella Choir under the direction of Charles F. Meys. He was also the director of the choir at Assumption Church at that time. Mr. Meys needed some singers for the church choir that year, and he asked some of the seniors to sing at the 12:15 Mass on Sundays. We did this for many months, loved doing it, and thought we were wonderful...I'm not sure what the congregation thought. But we loved it, and it remains a very happy memory for me."

Jane Rauscher Bardes
Parishioner since the 1930s

"I joined Assumption as a young child in the 1930s. My memories are of a typical pre-Vatican II parish: priest with his back to the people saying Mass in Latin with a few people following in English in the Missal, but most saying their rosaries or private prayers. It was a "pay, pray, and obey" church, a clerical culture exemplified by the altar rail which separated the priest from the people both physically and symbolically. There were only altar boys and no lay people in the sanctuary. It was an ethnically Irish parish; no diversity in people or perspectives; no outreach to the larger community; a rigid, separatist (ghetto) mentality.

"Along came Pope John XXIII and the Second Vatican Council. The windows flew open, allowing the Spirit to renew and refresh the Church. Now we have an open sanctuary, signifying the unity of the people of God, inviting and welcoming everyone. Now we all participate with the priest in offering the Mass in English. We have altar servers, both boys and girls. We are a warm, diverse community of believers with numerous ministries, using the talents of parishioners to minister to the needs of both the parish and the larger community. We are the Body of Christ being Christ to others."

Bernice Anglin
Parishioner since the 1930s

"I remember the wonderful fund-raising card parties we ran in the old school gym, which was then located behind the church. Sometimes the Mothers' Guild had responsibility for preparations, and we did that in the very tiny and crowded kitchen just off the gym. How hard we laughed! Those card parties held good times because we women got together playing and sharing experiences and stories. It became a card party without cards. Conversation and fellowship became far more important than the games, and the few serious players became a bit upset with us as we laughed and visited about anything but the cards. There were any number of us raising and educating our children in the Catholic tradition at the parish school, and we became good friends. Many of us have remained in the parish, grown old in the parish, and continue to love Assumption."

Joan Kramer
Parishioner since 1954

"We moved to Morristown in 1954 and joined Assumption immediately as we had a new baby to baptize. Father Doogan was pastor, and the church was beautiful. It had a beautiful main altar across the front of the church, altar rails, and two side altars. In all honesty, I wish the altar had been saved. To me it was part of our history, and we could have left it intact and still met the needs of the changes. At that time there were many statues of various saints that I believe were removed when the church was renovated after the fire. The Blessed Mother stained glass window behind the altar was and still is my main focus today.

"The school was still in the parking lot with the big bell that was the privilege of an eighth-grader to ring at noon. The school had a very good reputation and was the site for many social functions. Dances and card parties were held there as well as meetings. In the beginning, Father Doogan was not too happy to see us dancing on his new gym floor, but we soon discovered that, if we brought him a bottle of Irish whiskey and had a drink with him, he had as good a time as everyone else. When he retired, he would say Mass at one of the side altars, and my oldest son, Dave, who was one of the few young boys who still remembered Latin, would serve as his altar boy. When Father died, he left Dave his watch and cuff links.

"When Father Dericks was pastor, the first lay board was started. Looking back on those days, I feel really sorry for Father. Priests were used to running a church without the invasion of the laity. We burst on the scene ready to take over. There must be a record of all the chairmen somewhere, and we were all elected by the congregation.

"We were allowed home Masses. These were very special occasions. I had my first grandchild baptized at home, and my youngest made his First Communion at home before the church ceremony. CFM [Christian Family Movement] had home Masses for our group. It was always very special to have family and close friends together in one room for Mass.

"Another activity we all enjoyed were the Assumption picnics at Seton Hackney. We would get volunteers to get the games, someone to bring the keg of beer, baseballs and bats for a good game, and of course food. We all brought much of our own, but we had places to grill hot dogs and hamburgers. I felt at the time there was a divide between the public school kids and Assumption kids, but we did our best to include all in our plans and activities.

"The fire was the saddest event we lived through. David was mayor and was called by the fire department when it started. He could not go and watch and did not want me to go either."

Pat Manahan
Parishioner since 1954

"When I was three years old, my parents, my older sister, and I moved to Morristown from the Philadelphia area. I attended the new Assumption School through eighth grade and in about 1965 received the honor of being named Altar Boy of the Year, more for my willingness to serve early-morning weekday Masses than for my mastery of Latin. In 1973, I joined the Assumption Theater Group where I designed and built stage sets. Shortly after, I also joined the Assumption choir and remained a member for about five years. I was accepted into the U.S. Peace Corps in 1989 and served for two years as an agricultural volunteer in Sierra Leone, West Africa. My desire to help the people of Sierra Leone led me to revisit the country after their civil war ended in 2001, and I began to facilitate surgical treatments for some of those in need.

"Without the support I have received from the clergy and the parishioners of Assumption parish, it is unlikely that my efforts to make medical care and surgical treatments available to impoverished persons in Sierra Leone would have met with much success. Monsignor Martin Rauscher wrote a check in 2003 to pay for the first surgeries to treat ten men suffering with debilitating hernias. Father Martin also made the church available for fund-raising concerts which were attended by many Assumption parishioners. He elevated my work to the level of a parish ministry called Africa Surgery and allowed me to address the congregation after each Mass on one Sunday a year. He then provided Africa Surgery with an office in the Parish Ministry Center where he also provided me with convenient living quarters. Monsignor John Hart continues to allow Africa Surgery to play its role as a part of Assumption Parish—he and Father Dennis Crowley highly praising our work whenever Africa

Surgery is mentioned in the altar announcements. Their words never fall on deaf ears nor fail to move the generous hearts of Assumption parishioners, for which I and the scores of people healed and helped in Sierra Leone are forever grateful."

Tom Johnson, Jr.
Director, Africa Surgery Ministry
Parishioner since 1955

"In August of 1960, my husband Dave and I moved to Morristown along with six children plus a seventh on the way. We joined Assumption when Father Doogan was pastor and enrolled the children in Assumption School. We became actively involved in the Home and School group where Dave became president. Working with Jo Doyle, Joycelyn Rigassio, Josephine Preziosi, and others, we held many activities such as card parties and an annual spaghetti dinner—and so began the tradition of our fashion show.

"Father Dericks became the new pastor and began many new programs. We became part of the pastoral council, and Dave became a Trustee. As Eucharistic Ministers we took communion to shut-ins and nursing homes. The school continued to grow and became, as it is today, one of the best in the diocese.

"One memory that stays in my mind is the electrical fire that burned the church. After much hard work under the direction of Father Michael Conway, the church was beautifully restored. During the restoration, Masses were held at the school, and it became a time when we all came together.

"In 1990 Father Martin Rauscher became pastor. He did a superb job of bringing everyone together. We started an annual dinner with a 50/50 raffle. There were many ministries formed and a new parish center was added to the back of the church. We had frequent 'coffee and...' after Masses. After nineteen years, Father Martin retired but not before he had the church restored to its original beauty. He left a wonderful legacy.

"The parish is a wonderful community of people where all are welcome. As a family, we have experienced personally the love and support from other members of the parish and the school where I have been privileged to teach for so many years.

"I am most proud of what Assumption has done in its long history. It continues to help people in the community, especially the poor, whether they are Catholic or not. How fortunate we are to be part of this wonderful, caring parish."

Irene Phelan
Parishioner since 1960

"I joined the parish late in 1974 when a job transfer took me to New Jersey after a move from New York. It turned out to be a really good move for me in every way. Joining Assumption was a very significant part of those positive feelings. The warmth of the reception I received made me feel a part of the Assumption family from the very first day. That hospitality I experienced has a long history at Assumption and is very much alive and well today! We are truly blessed to be part of this wonderful vibrant Christian community."

Dot McDonough
Parishioner since 1974

"Assumption has played a very special role in our lives: we met and married at Assumption and Bob buried his mother from Assumption. Bob joined the parish in 1968; Jeanette in 1979, having moved from the Midwest in a career advancement invitation from AT&T. When Bob first arrived at Assumption in the spring of 1968, he had his mother with him, as they were in the process of relocating to Morristown from Staten Island. Monsignor Dericks had just been named pastor. The church was dark and gloomy; plaster was hanging off the walls; obviously much work needed to be done to the physical plant. When they returned in the fall after having completed the move to Morristown, it was as if a transformation had taken place. The church was bright and cheerful—it had been painted!

"In the late Sixties and early Seventies, there were still many parishioners from 'the Old Country'; that is, the 'Old Sod' of Ireland. Being of Irish extraction, (Bob's mother's maiden name was McCarthy), they felt at home.

"We met at an Assumption choir rehearsal in 1983. The then-Minister of Music Kevin Norris introduced us. We sang together in the church choir, began dating, and were married by Monsignor Dericks in July 1984. What better place can one meet one's future spouse? We joke that Assumption was our dating service.

"Our reason for writing this history of our great parish is that this story is indeed One for the Books. Our parish established formal education in Morristown years before the Town of Morristown set up its own, established All Souls Hospital in Morristown years before the advent of Morristown Memorial Hospital, and is the mother church of several of the parishes in the southeastern part of Morris County. These are just a few of the great contributions made by our parish. Truly this is a story that needs to be shared with the community and diocese at large.

"God has blessed us with the energy and health to remain active in parish life, for which we are very grateful. We love Assumption and its parish community and have made many good friends here. We will remain an active part of it as long as God so wills."

Bob and Jeanette Fredericks
Bob, Parishioner since 1968
Jeanette, Parishioner since 1979

"We joined Assumption [as single people]: Bruno in June 1986 when he moved from New York City to Morristown; Theresa in July 1986 when she moved from Parsippany to Morristown. We were both widowed and each bought townhouses in the Windmill Pond development in Morristown, two doors from each other. We casually met as neighbors and eventually became good friends. We had similar family backgrounds, and we both believed that we were meant for each other. We felt that God had a hand in it.

"We were married on February 14, 1993, by Monsignor Martin Rauscher. We plan to remain faithful members of our favorite church—Assumption of the Blessed Virgin Mary."

Bruno and Theresa DiPaolo
Parishioners since 1986

"After having belonged to the same parish on Staten Island for many years, Richard and I didn't know what to expect when we moved to Morris Township and joined Assumption Church. We immediately felt at home because of the warm welcome we received from everyone: Father Martin, Father Dennis, Sister Pat, Sister Marie, the deacons, office staff, and parishioners. Since we became parishioners, we have participated in the many opportunities provided to expand and deepen our faith. Richard and I thank God for the wonderful spiritual journey afforded us through the faithful, dedicated community at Assumption."

Richard and Marianna Quagliano
Parishioners since 2000

the
PARISH
MILESTONES

BAPTISMS &
MARRIAGES

Milestones in the History of our Parish

August 15, 1848

The first Catholic church in Morristown, originally named St. Mary's Church and later renamed the Church of the Assumption of the Blessed Virgin Mary, was dedicated.

December 25, 1848

The first Mass was celebrated in the newly constructed Church of the Assumption of the Blessed Virgin Mary.

1850

Saint Mary's School, the forerunner of Assumption School, was established in the basement of the first church, with 25 pupils.

1861

The first rectory was constructed during the pastorate of Father Hoey. Located in what is now the upper parking lot, it was enlarged and modified many times, eventually becoming the Bayley High School.

June 30, 1872

The cornerstone of our current church was laid.

May 22, 1873

Bishop Michael Corrigan of Newark dedicated the current church.

September 1875

Sisters of Charity of Saint Elizabeth took charge of St. Mary's School (later to be renamed the Bayley School and still later Assumption School).

Spring 1875

Sixteen acres were purchased in Morris Township, to become Holy Rood Cemetery.

1881

The steeple bell, named "Saint Patrick," was acquired and installed.

October 19, 1881

Bishop Winand Wigger blessed the bell "Saint Patrick." It continues to ring in our steeple to this day.

September 19, 1887

St. Mary's School was opened as a stand-alone structure, later to be renamed The Bayley School.

1887

The current Stations of the Cross were installed in the church.

May 1, 1888

The Young Men's Catholic Association building was constructed on South Street as a home for this organization, formed in 1881. This structure is currently the headquarters of the George Washington Council of the Knights of Columbus.

1890

The present rectory was constructed; it was occupied on November 25.

1892

All Souls Hospital commenced operations.

1916

The Ballantine estate at the corner of Macculloch Avenue and Perry Street was purchased to serve as the parish convent; it is now the Ministry Center.

1948

The Walker estate in Madison, which became the site of the Bayley-Ellard High School and is now a diocesan evangelical center, "St. Paul Inside the Walls," was bequeathed to Assumption.

June 7, 1949

The Parker estate on Macculloch Avenue was purchased to serve as the future Assumption School, which was formally dedicated on March 17, 1957.

1976

Construction began on the first of four mausoleums at Holy Rood Cemetery.

April 10, 1985

The church was almost destroyed by fire.

December 24, 1986

The reconstructed church reopened.

1994

The Parish Center was completed and blessed.

Baptisms and Marriages
Conducted at Assumption
1856 through 2010

YEARS	BAPTISMS	MARRIAGES
1856 – 1859	*200*	*55*
1860 – 1869	*579*	*120*
1870 – 1879	*704*	*147*
1880 – 1889	*679*	*141*
1890 – 1899	*1,098*	*225*
1900 – 1909	*1,272*	*225*
1910 – 1919	*1,598*	*380*
1920 – 1929	*1,639*	*506*
1930 – 1939	*740*	*315*
1940 – 1949	*887*	*315*
1950 – 1959	*1,544*	*377*
1960 – 1969	*1,723*	*338*
1970 – 1979	*658*	*258*
1980 – 1989	*943*	*375*
1990 – 1999	*1,571*	*751*
2000 – 2010	*1,886*	*600*
TOTAL	*17,721*	*5,128*

the
REFERENCES

List of Works Consulted or Cited

Beers, F.W., A.B. Prindle, et al. *Atlas of Morris County, New Jersey, 1868.*
F.W. Beers, A.D. Ellis & G.G. Soule, New York, 1868. Reprinted by the Morris
County Historical Society, 1984

Cavanaugh, Cam. *In Lights and Shadows: Morristown in Three Centuries.* The Joint
Free Public Library of Morristown and Morris Township, Morristown, New Jersey,
1986

Church of the Assumption. Custom Books, Inc., Hackensack, New Jersey, 1972 and
1976

Cunningham, John T., The Morris Educational Foundation. *Youth's Bright Years:
An American High School, Morristown, New Jersey.* Bookcrafters, Inc., USA, 1999

"Dedication Program, Assumption of the B.V.M. School, March 17, 1957."
L.P. Thebault Company, Morristown, New Jersey, 1957

Flynn, Joseph M., MR, RD *Story of a Parish, 1847-1892.* Columbus Press, New York,
1892

Flynn, Joseph M., MR, VF *The Catholic Church in New Jersey.* Press of the
Publishers Printing Company, New York, 1904

Godri, Pat, SC, Research Editor. "Compilation of Historical Data from 1698-1994,
Church of the Assumption of the B.V.M."

Hoffman, Philip H. *History of the Arnold Tavern, Morristown, New Jersey.*
Chronicle Press, Morristown, New Jersey, 1903

Kupke, PhD, Rev. Raymond. *Living Stones: A History of the Catholic Church in the
Diocese of Paterson.* Walsworth Printing, Marceline, Missouri, 1987

Mahoney, Joseph F. and Peter J. Wosh, Editors. *The Diocesan Journal of Michael
Augustine Corrigan, Bishop of Newark, 1872-1880.* New Jersey Historical Society and
the New Jersey Catholic Historical Records Commission, 1987

Miekam, Rev. Albert R. *One Hundredth Anniversary, Church of the Assumption of the B.V.M, 1848-1949.* Colyer Printing Company, Newark, New Jersey, 1949

Munsell, W. W., Editors. *History of Morris County 1739-1882.* W. W. Munsell and Company, New York, 1882. Reprinted by the Morris County Historical Society, 1973

"Parish Bulletins, Church of the Assumption." 1966-2010

Parish Review, The Official Organ of the Church of the Assumption. August 1937

"Property Transfers," *The Jerseyman.* May 10, 1916

Sheeran, Rev. James, CSSR. *Confederate Chaplain: A War Journal.* Bruce Publishing Company, Milwaukee, Wisconsin, 1960

Sisters of Charity of Saint Elizabeth. *Caritas. Sisters of Charity, Convent Station, New Jersey, 1859-1959.* New City Printing Co., Union City, New Jersey

Stained Glass Window Order Records, Hiemer & Co., Clifton, New Jersey, 1955-1956, 1958, and 2004

Stained Glass Window Shipping Records, Mayer & Co., Munich, Germany, 1882-1906

We Remember, We Celebrate, We Believe, 150 Years. PCA International, Inc., Matthews, North Carolina, 1998

Yearbooks of Assumption Grade School
   School Annual Publishing, Coshhocton, Ohio, 1978
   Taylor Publishing Company, Dallas, Texas, 2005

List of Individuals Interviewed for this Publication

Anglin, Bernice *

Casey, Father Joe *

Duffy, Monsignor Francis

Fleming, Mary Kay and John *

Godri, Sister Pat (SC)

Harty, Bill and Claire *

Kramer, Joan *

Hoyt, Helen *

Larkin, Sister Merris (SC)

Lasch, Monsignor Kenneth *

McMahon, Lorraine

Morrissey, Sister June (SC)

Murphy, Sister Kathleen (Mary Roseaire, SC)

Phelan, Irene *

Rauscher, Monsignor Martin *

Smith, Mary Louise Hallinan *

Interview recorded for Assumption Oral History Library

Photograph and Service Credits

Bernardsville Public Library, Local History Department

Burani, Sergio—Photos by Sergio *(Photography for Philanthropy)*

Kupke, Monsignor Raymond *(liturgical and historical editing services)*

Kurlander, Karen Ann *(proofreading and copy editing services)*

Lawless, Fred and Mary Alice *(archival photographs and videos)*

McLaughlin, Sister Elizabeth (SC), Archivist, Sisters of Charity, Convent Station, NJ

Morris County Hall of Records

Morris County Library, Local History and Genealogy Department

Mullaney, Kenneth, General Counsel, Diocese of Paterson *(review services)*

Olson, Eric, Morristown National Historical Park

Smith, Mary Louise *(personal collection)*

Stanton, Norma *(personal collection)*

Turkington, Cheryl, Assistant Archivist, North Jersey History and
Genealogy Center of the Morristown & Morris Township Library